CHAUVET CAVE

THE DISCOVERY OF THE WORLD'S OLDEST PAINTINGS

Jean-Marie Chauvet
Eliette Brunel Deschamps
Christian Hillaire

CHAUVET CAVE

THE DISCOVERY OF THE WORLD'S OLDEST PAINTINGS

Foreword by Paul G. Bahn
Epilogue by Jean Clottes

With 93 colour illustrations

 Thames & Hudson

The accounts by Jean-Marie Chauvet, Eliette Brunel Deschamps and
Christian Hillaire were obtained by Séverine Nikel

Translated from the French *La Grotte Chauvet* by Paul G. Bahn

First published in the United Kingdom in 1996 by Thames & Hudson Ltd,
181A High Holborn, London WC1V 7QX

First paperback edition 2001
www.thamesandhudson.com

British Library Cataloguing-in-Publication Data
A catalogue record for this book is available from the British Library

ISBN 0-500-28286-2

Printed and bound in France

CONTENTS

FOREWORD
Paul G. Bahn

I was travelling abroad on 18 January 1995 when the news of the discovery of Chauvet Cave hit the media, and my initial reaction on seeing the first pictures of the amazing rhinos and big cats was that this might be a fake: they were simply too stunning and too unusual to fit the picture we have built up of Ice Age cave art over the past century. But as soon as I learned who had found the cave, I realized that it must be the real thing. I had the good fortune to visit some of the decorated Ardèche caves in the autumn of 1993 with Jean-Marie Chauvet and Eliette Brunel Deschamps, and I knew them to be true specialists, wholly dedicated to the discovery and study of the priceless underground heritage of their beautiful region. It was no surprise to me at all that, having made their spectacular discovery, they and their friend Christian Hillaire took the utmost care to preserve it as intact as possible for future generations. The procedure they adopted was exemplary and one hopes that, through this book, it will become widely known and hence adopted by all future discoverers of sites of this kind.

The initial suspicion of fakery has become almost automatic in the world of Ice Age art. There have been many cases of counterfeit portable art objects in the past and it is disturbing to reflect that some world-famous examples of Ice Age art – unearthed long ago and without any real archaeological provenance, at a time when labourers were often paid by the find – may well be fakes, so that our knowledge of true Ice Age art has become distorted by having such objects entrenched in the accepted corpus. It may never be possible to weed them out, especially if they were made on stone or genuine fossil ivory, for example. Cases of fakery in cave art are less common, but they have been known and can sometimes be detected. The most recent example is that of Zubialde, in the Spanish Basque country. Photographs of the paintings in this cave appeared in the European press in March 1991, and most specialists immediately smelt a rat – not only were the animals depicted highly unusual for Spain (rhino, mammoth), and some of the 'signs' quite bizarre, but a few animals such as the bison were very ugly and clumsily executed. However, none of these features by itself is sufficient grounds for dismissing a new site, and the narrowness of the cave had clearly distorted some of the figures in the photographs. Zubialde was initially believed to be authentic by a handful of eminent Spanish specialists, and was reported in the popular archaeological literature. It required scientific analysis of the pigments – found to contain highly perishable materials such as insect legs, as well as synthetic fibres from modern kitchen sponges – to prove that it was a forgery.

It was therefore with Zubialde fresh in their minds that some specialists – myself included – were initially highly sceptical of Cosquer Cave, announced only a few months later, with its colourful discoverer, its unprecedented geographical location, its entrance beneath the Mediterranean – so reminiscent of the plot of Hammond Innes' novel *Levkas Man* – and its unusual drawings such as the great auks, the 'jellyfish', the atypical hand stencils and the bison drawn three-quarter face. All these strange artistic traits were featured in the limited range of photographs which the world's press chose to publish. Had they deigned to print photographs showing the numerous engravings, or the calcited finger markings, the situation would have been different. As it was, the sight of good-quality photographs of the whole range of the Cosquer figures had convinced everyone of its authenticity well before the art was subjected to radiocarbon dating.

As Jean Clottes comments in his 'Epilogue', no such doubts assailed Chauvet Cave, for many reasons – the quantity and sophistication of the figures, the quality of the photographs given to the press, the impeccable testimony and credentials of the discoverers and the subsequent verification by specialists. But the small cave of La Covaciella, discovered in Asturias (northern Spain) in late 1994, did arouse the usual doubts: its bison paintings were so well preserved, and one Spanish specialist assured me that he had strong misgivings about its authenticity because one figure was the identical twin of a well-known bison at Santimamiñe, even to the extent of being produced with the same number of strokes. Despite these doubts, however, charcoal in the Covaciella bison figures has now been directly dated to more than 14,000 years ago. It is extremely improbable – though, of course, not impossible – that modern fakers could have obtained sufficient charcoal of that period to produce these drawings.

So doubts still arise where figures are clumsy or ugly (as at Zubialde, justifiably), where they are too different in technique or content from what we already know (as at Cosquer), or, conversely, where they are too similar to what we know (as at La Covaciella, and, ironically, at Cosquer again where some figures were thought by some to have been copied from Lascaux and other caves). Scepticism is always healthy, but at the same time the new discoveries – especially Chauvet Cave – have taught us that our current knowledge of Ice Age art is highly incomplete and susceptible to profound modification. But that is true of many branches of archaeology, and exemplifies the fascination and excitement of a subject where a single find – be it a hominid bone, the Iceman, or a new cave – can cause all the text books to be rewritten.

Chauvet Cave was startling in many respects – no decorated cave of such size had ever been found in this part of France; it was completely intact, with its varied traces of human and animal visitors (including the already notorious bear skull placed on a rock, which has led to so much speculation about bear cults, but could just as easily be explained by a bored child playing in the cave while the adults were painting!); and it had so many images of so many different species, most notably rhinoceroses, big cats and bears – animals that were not only hitherto unknown in this region's Ice Age art, but were also rare anywhere else, and certainly not usually depicted with such prominence on main panels. For example, less than twenty rhinos were previously known in European cave art, whereas Chauvet alone contains between two and three times that many. However, it is the direct dates from three of the cave's figures which, as Jean Clottes explains later, have really revolutionized our view of Ice Age art.

The Dating of Palaeolithic Cave Art

In the past, proof of the Palaeolithic age of cave art took many forms: for example, the depiction of animals which are now extinct (such as mammoth), or which were present only during the Ice Age (such as figures of reindeer in southern France and northern Spain) first served to convince the scientific world of the reality of Ice Age art. Quite a few caves were blocked during or just after the Ice Age – for example, since occupation deposits of the Palaeolithic period blocked and masked the decorated gallery at La Mouthe (Dordogne), it was obvious that any art in the gallery had to date to the last Ice Age. Similar proof occurs in cases where all or part of the decorated walls themselves are covered by Palaeolithic deposits (datable through their bone and stone tools, or through radiocarbon dating of organic material). In a few sites, fragments of decorated wall have fallen and become stratified in the archaeological layer.

All such occurrences provide a minimum age for the cave art, whereas at some sites in high valleys, such as Niaux and Fontanet in the French Pyrenees, occupation cannot have taken place before the mid-Magdalenian (c. 15,500 years ago) because of glacial activity, so this gives one a maximum age for the art.

If a cave contains evidence of Palaeolithic occupation, it has usually been assumed that its wall art belongs to the same period, though this is by no means always certain. One example, however, where the assumption appears reliable is La Tête-du-Lion (Ardèche), where charcoal fragments in a fireplace lay next to some spots of red ochre on the ground. Analysis proved the ochre to be of exactly the same composition as that in the aurochs painting on the wall above, and the radiocarbon date of 21,650 BP (before the present) from the charcoal may therefore provide a fairly reliable age for the art.

A different type of artistic evidence from a site's occupation layers is portable art. In some sites which contain both wall art and portable art (such as Altamira or El Castillo in Santander) one can see clear analogies between the two in technique and style. However, if a decorated cave was unoccupied or has no portable art, the only recourse until very recently was to seek stylistic comparisons with material from other sites and even other regions. This inevitably led to problems of subjectivity and over-simplistic schemes of development. All stylistic arguments are based on an assumption that figures which appear similar in style or technique were roughly contemporaneous in their execution.

The first major scheme put forward for the development of cave art was that of the abbé Henri Breuil, the French cleric who dominated cave art studies from their inception until his death in 1961. He based much of his scheme on the presence or absence of 'twisted perspective', a feature he considered primitive, which means that an animal figure in profile still has its horns, antlers, tusks or hoofs facing the front. Breuil's view was inconsistent, since twisted perspective is also known in the Magdalenian (for example in the hoofs of the bison on the famous ceiling of Altamira), while true perspective was already known in early phases (as in some ibex figures at Gargas). Twisted perspective, therefore, was never a reliable chronological marker.

Breuil saw Palaeolithic art as developing in two successive cycles, the 'Aurignaco-Perigordian' and the 'Solutreo-Magdalenian'. These similar but independent cycles of evolution each progressed from simple to complex forms, starting with 'primitive' or archaic figures, and leading on to more complex and detailed images. There was an overall progression from schematic to naturalistic and finally degenerate forms.

This scheme was eventually superseded by that of André Leroi-Gourhan, the French prehistorian who in turn dominated cave art studies until his death in 1986. He concentrated primarily on the characteristics of what seemed to be securely dated figures (both wall art and portable art). He proposed a series of four 'styles' which, unlike Breuil's cycles, were seen as an unbroken development with a series of 'pushes' separated by long periods of transition. Style I comprised material from the Aurignacian and early Gravettian (c. 40,000–25,000 years ago) – notably carved blocks with deeply incised motifs, fallen fragments of decorated walls, crude figures with stiff contours, and wall art only in daylight areas of caves and shelters. Style II, covering the rest of the Gravettian and part of the Solutrean (*c.* 25,000–20,000 years ago), featured good animal profiles with a sinuous neck/back line, often an elongated head, and twisted perspective, but with the extremities of the limbs rarely depicted. It contained far more portable art (such as the 'Venus' figurines) than wall art, the latter still being restricted to daylight zones. Style III, spanning the rest of the Solutrean and the early Magdalenian (*c.* 20,000–15,000 years ago) was characterized by the animal figures in caves such as Lascaux and Pech Merle, with undersized heads and limbs, and semi-twisted perspective dominating. Leroi-Gourhan believed that decoration of the dark parts of the caves began in this phase. Finally, Style IV contained all the wonders of mid- and late-Magdalenian art (*c.* 15,000–10,000 years ago), with the decoration of really deep galleries, and the gradual appearance of lively, animated figures.

Leroi-Gourhan's scheme, therefore, was fundamentally like Breuil's in that, from a modern viewpoint, it saw an overall progression from simple, archaic forms to complex, detailed, accurate figures of animals, and treated Palaeolithic art as an essentially uniform phenomenon. Diversity was played down in favour of standardization, and the development was greatly oversimplified.

It is easy to be wise with hindsight, and to criticize these schemes now that we have more and better evidence at our disposal. Nevertheless, long before the first results from direct dating of cave art became available, many specialists had grown dissatisfied with Leroi-Gourhan's scheme, and independently reached the conclusion that Palaeolithic art did not have a single beginning and a single climax. There must have been many of both, varying from region to region and from period to period. Within those 30,000 years or more, there must obviously have been periods of stagnation, improvement, and even regression,

with different influences, innovations, experiments and discoveries coming into play. The development of Palaeolithic art was probably akin to evolution itself – not a straight line or a ladder, but a much more circuitous path, a complex growth like a bush, with occasional flashes of brilliance. Art is, after all, produced by individual artists, and the sporadic appearance of genius during this timespan cannot really be fitted into a general scheme. Each period of the Palaeolithic almost certainly saw the co-existence and fluctuating importance of a number of styles and techniques (both realistic and schematic), as well as a wide range of talent and ability (not forgetting the different styles and degrees of skill through which any Palaeolithic Picasso will have passed in a lifetime). There must have been different developments at different times in different regions, and similar styles in two separate regions are not necessarily contemporaneous.

Leroi-Gourhan fully admitted that not every apparently 'primitive' or 'archaic' figure is necessarily old, and, conversely, that some of the earliest art would probably look quite sophisticated. Nevertheless, he failed to take full advantage of the data that was already available to him. For example, he neglected the hundreds of pieces of well-dated portable art from the eastern Spanish cave of Parpalló, perhaps because they displayed a number of features that contradicted his scheme; and in particular, he was perplexed by the sophisticated ivory carvings from the southwest German Aurignacian, such as the Vogelherd animals, and placed them in his Style II, thus denying their actual provenance. As Jean Clottes points out in this book, it is the presence of sophisticated carvings like these in Germany, together with the astonishing 'Dancing Venus' of Galgenberg in Austria, all of them more than 30,000 years old, which should have prepared us for the very early date and the tremendous sophistication of Chauvet Cave's wall paintings and engravings. Far from representing the early, crude fumblings of the first artists, the

Aurignacian clearly displays a phenomenon that had already been in existence for a very long time.

Radiocarbon dates

The direct dating of cave art has become possible thanks to two different advances. First, the analysis of the paints used has been improved enormously. At the turn of the century, when such analyses began, they could only be carried out by chemical reaction, and the first results obtained – iron oxide for red, manganese dioxide for black – were assumed to be the standard for all cave art. However, the development in recent years of new techniques such as scanning electron microscopy, X-ray diffraction and proton-induced X-ray emission has meant that extremely detailed and accurate assessments of paint contents and composition have become possible, and it has been established that the black substance used in cave art is usually charcoal. This was first identified at Niaux fifteen years ago, but charcoal has turned up in almost every black figure analyzed since then, in old caves and new. (One can speculate that manganese dioxide was used by the faker at Zubialde in order to avoid the possibility of direct dating, but it is equally likely that the faker still believed the textbook view that this mineral was what Palaeolithic artists always used, and was unaware of the newly discovered ubiquity of charcoal!) The second advance has been the introduction of Accelerator Mass Spectrometry. In the past, even if the presence of organic material had been known in cave art, it would have been unacceptable to date figures directly, since the large amount of charcoal required for radiocarbon dating would have destroyed the entire figure. The AMS technique, on the other hand, requires only a minute quantity of charcoal, so tiny that its removal does not affect the figure.

Direct dates have been obtained so far from figures in nine European Ice Age caves – three in northern Spain and six in southern France. They are presented in the chart on p. 131. By and large they confirm the ages which had been estimated for these caves on the basis of style and archaeological material, but some surprises have also turned up – most notably at Chauvet, as Jean Clottes explains below, though even here the early dates tally well with the sophisticated portable imagery known from this period in south-west Germany and elsewhere. But whereas stylistic studies had assigned the art in the cave of Cougnac to about 18,000–16,000 years ago, the charcoal in dots on the wall points to a later period, while dates for the cave's figures of the extinct giant deer are several millennia earlier, from 19,500 to 25,120 years ago.

Similar results have emerged from the cave of Niaux in the French Pyrenees. A number of different mixtures of pigments and minerals have been detected. In Niaux's famous 'Salon Noir' sanctuary, most of the animal figures were first sketched in charcoal, with manganese paint added on top. This was clearly a special place where the figures were carefully planned, whereas the other figures in the cave were done without preliminary sketches. In the past, the whole of Niaux's decoration was assigned on stylistic grounds to about 14,000 years ago; however, charcoal from two bison figures in the 'Salon Noir' has now been radiocarbon dated and produced strikingly different results: one bison was dated to 13,850 years ago, as expected, but the other produced a date of 12,890 years ago: in other words, Niaux's decoration seems to have been built up in at least two separate phases.

In Spain, charcoal was discovered in some of the bison paintings from the cave of Altamira: three of them have been dated, and produced results that average out at about 14,000 years ago. However, similar paintings from the nearby cave of El Castillo were dated to about 12,990 years ago, a millennium later than expected.

A number of important points need to be stressed in relation to all the direct dates obtained so far from cave art. First, what has been dated is the death of the tree that produced the charcoal, which is not necessarily the same as the time when the charcoal was used to produce the figure: in most cases the two events are probably not very far apart, but it is theoretically possible that people could have entered a cave and used charcoal from an ancient hearth to draw on the walls, so the charcoal's age represents merely a maximum age for the art. Second, the figures produced by the laboratories and listed on p. 131 – even if they are all accurate and free of contamination, which is a considerable assumption since even minute contamination can produce great distortion – are uncalibrated radiocarbon ages, not precise calendar dates. The plus/minus figure after the main figure indicates that the true age has a 68% chance of being within that time span; to attain an accuracy of 95% one has to double this span. Third, a single date is of little use or reliability, and it is unfortunate that some of the dated figures can never be redated owing to lack of usable organic material. As Jean Clottes points out, if just one date of 30,000 years had been obtained for Chauvet Cave, nobody would have believed the result; it was the series of dates, together with the more recent figures obtained for torch marks on top of the calcite that covered

the art, which convinced everyone of the art's antiquity despite the universal amazement.

Nevertheless, these uncertainties and caveats concerning radiocarbon dates are – and always have been – equally applicable to the rest of the archaeological record. Because of the '68% chance', it is obvious that at least a third of radiocarbon dates may be faulty; some are recognized as such immediately, because they are so incongruous, but others that are currently accepted as correct are probably wrong. The study of the archaeological record by means of the radiocarbon method is still being improved and refined. In the meantime we have to make do with the results currently obtained, however imperfect they may be and whatever their limitations; despite the growing list, the dated figures are, of course, only a very tiny fraction of the cave art corpus. However, it is certain that over the next few years many more dates will be obtained for images in cave art which will help specialists to fine-tune their knowledge of how, when and perhaps even why these sites were decorated in this way. It is equally certain that Chauvet Cave will play a significant role in all future studies of the art not only of Europe but of the world.

Map showing the decorated cave sites mentioned in the text.

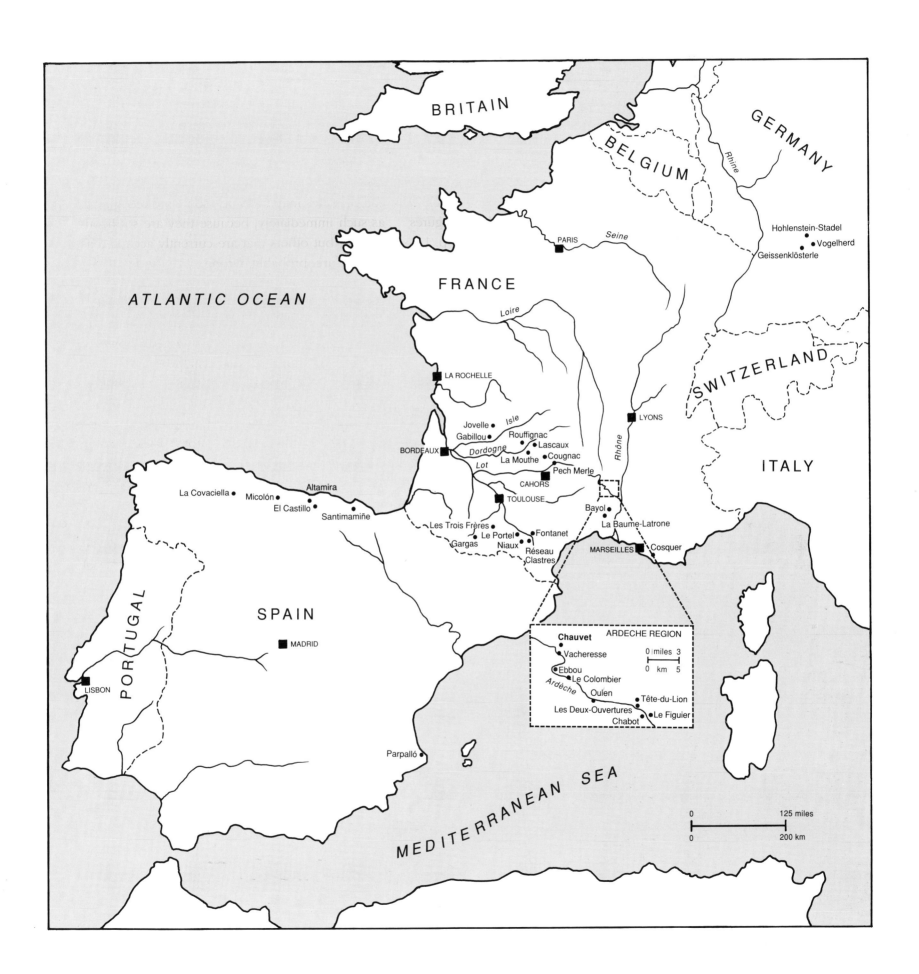

BRITAIN

GERMANY

BELGIUM

Rhine

ATLANTIC OCEAN

■ PARIS

Seine

FRANCE

Hohlenstein-Stadel
• Vogelherd
• Geissenklösterle

Loire

■ LA ROCHELLE

■ LYONS

SWITZERLAND

Jovelle •   *Isle*
Gabillou •   Rouffignac •
BORDEAUX ■   • Lascaux
Dordogne   La Mouthe • • Cougnac
Lot   Pech Merle •
CAHORS ■

Rhône

ITALY

La Covaciella •   Altamira
Micolón •   •
El Castillo •   • • TOULOUSE
Santimamiñe •   Bayol •
Les Trois Frères •   La Baume-Latrone •
Gargas • Le Portel • • Fontanet
• Niaux
Réseau   MARSEILLES ■ • Cosquer
Clastres •

PORTUGAL

SPAIN

■ MADRID

ARDÈCHE REGION

Chauvet
• Vacheresse

0 ┃ miles 3
0 ┃ km 5

Ardèche   Ebbou ● •
• Le Colombier
Oulen •   • Tête-du-Lion
Les Deux-Ouvertures •   • Le Figuier
Chabot •

■ LISBON

• Parpalló

MEDITERRANEAN SEA

0
├──────────────┤ 125 miles
0
├──────────────┤ 200 km

THE DISCOVERY OF CHAUVET CAVE

On the evening of 18 December 1994 we were the first three people for perhaps twenty thousand years to set foot in one of the world's most beautiful decorated caves: Chauvet Cave. Located in the side of a cliff in the gorges of the Ardèche in south-east France, it lies in the heart of a region that we have been exploring for many years.

THE GORGES OF THE ARDECHE

The three of us grew up in this beautiful region, and we love its wild, dry and rocky landscapes. The plateaux and limestone masses of the southern Ardèche are covered in vines, fields of lavender, moorland or heath, a dry vegetation of Judas trees, evergreen oaks, boxtrees and Spanish junipers. In spring there is an odour of thyme, wild roses and honeysuckle. Soils are thin, and there are outcrops of grey rock everywhere.

Over a distance of more than 30 kilometres (20 miles) the Ardèche has cut vertiginous gorges, 100–200 metres (330–660 ft) deep, into the plateau of the Bas Vivarais. Between cliffs of sometimes dazzling whiteness, often blending with tints of grey and ochre, the river winds its way, rapidly or calmly, tracing great meanders or sharp bends. At the entrance to the gorges it has pierced the rock with a beautiful natural arch that spans the waters, the famous Pont d'Arc. In places, the escarpments overhang gentler scree slopes covered in dark green vegetation. The slightest terrace and the smallest level area on the flanks of the cliffs are invaded by trees and scrub. Since 1980 this site of wild beauty, to which tourists flock during the summer, has been classed as a nature reserve. All the animal and plant species as well as the landscape are protected here.

In the limestone plateau, innumerable cavities have been hollowed out by the waters infiltrating the rock, and are located in tiers at different levels in the cliff. Since the Palaeolithic period, and almost up to the present day, people have found refuge in them. The biggest, such as Oulen or Le Figuier, were turned into dwelling places in the Upper Palaeolithic; others were used as burial caves. In a great many of them, since the turn of the century, archaeologists have unearthed traces of the past – flints, ornaments,

Double page overleaf:
1. The cliffs of the Cirque d'Estre at the entrance of the gorges of the Ardèche. Chauvet Cave is at the foot of the highest cliff.

15

2. Jean-Marie Chauvet taking a topographic reading.

3. Eliette Brunel Deschamps and Christian Hillaire emerging from a cavity after an exploration of the Charette swallowhole.

18

pottery, etc. Some caves were used as hiding places during the Religious Wars, and, up to the start of the twentieth century, they were occasionally occupied by charcoal burners and shepherds.

Since the end of the nineteenth century, twenty-eight decorated caves have been discovered in the gorges of the Ardèche (twelve of them by ourselves). Most of the known caves date from the Palaeolithic period known as the Solutrean (21,000–18,000 years ago) – for example, Chabot, Le Figuier, Oulen, La Tête-du-Lion, Les Deux-Ouvertures, and most of the depictions in Ebbou – while the two sites of Le Colombier are attributed to the Magdalenian (about 15,000 years ago). However, until the discovery of Chauvet Cave, the decorated caves of the Ardèche were considered a minor ensemble in comparison with the wall art of the Dordogne or the Pyrenees.

THE THREE DISCOVERERS

We have been speleologists for more than twenty years, and have long been familiar with the Mediterranean regions, particularly the Ardèche and Gard. We share the same taste for discovering unexplored galleries, for the beauty of the concretions and the strange forms of the mineral world. All of our free time is devoted to this shared passion, and we sometimes have to move tons of rubble and masses of earth to achieve results that may sometimes be disappointing, but which can at other times be grandiose. It is a fine reward, however, when we are the first people to enter a previously unknown cave, free from all blemishes, where a thousand lights sparkle in the beam of our torches.

We met each other through speleology and it was by searching together that our friendship was born – during the course of long explorations made memorable by the effort and emotion of discovery, and by shared jokes and laughter.

Eliette Brunel Deschamps

Eliette, who is a wine producer, was born in Saint-Remèze, a few kilometres from the gorges. She started caving at the age of eighteen when some friends took her along to the Spéléo-Club of Saint Marcel. Since then she has devoted all her leisure time to speleology. In the 1970s, while still a beginner, she and two friends cleared out a swallowhole – the Aven du Cade – on the plateau of Saint-Remèze, and discovered a prehistoric habitation at the bottom. With her friend, Bernadette Bénini, she has also done a great deal of exploration in the gorges of the Ardèche, where they have discovered two burial caves rich in archaeological material (over three thousand ornaments were unearthed in one cave, and several hundred in the other). When the three of us met, Eliette was interested in both archaeology and speleology, and, at the time of our introduction, it was certainly she who was best acquainted with the gorges and the paths down from the clifftops.

Jean-Marie Chauvet

Jean-Marie was born in Auvergne, but his parents settled in the Ardèche when he was five. He has been a speleologist since childhood. At the age of twelve, in an Ardèche cave, he practised caving with some friends, all of them wearing helmets from the Second World War. At this time he read Norbert Casteret's book *My Life Underground*, and was inspired by the idea of experiencing the same adventures as his hero. He will never forget his dazzled amazement on seeing a magnificent flow of white calcite for the first time, which took on fantastic proportions in the eyes of the child. A member of the Spéléo-Club des Vans since 1970, for a long time he practised cave diving, in particular exploring the Claysse system, and he has visited numerous caves in the Gard, the Lozère, the Causses and the Ardèche. Fascinated by wall art, he has made several trips with friends to the Tassili massif in Algeria, where they discovered three exceptional rock art sites. For twenty years he has been photographing the magnificent sites he has explored. He has been custodian of the decorated caves of the Ardèche since 1993.

Christian Hillaire

Christian is a technician at Pierrelatte, and was born at Pont-Saint-Esprit, in the Gard, on the right bank of the Ardèche. As a child, he recalls being attracted by these mysterious caves, which he could see from the river when he went down the gorges in a kayak. It was here that he was initiated into speleology, at La Goule de Foussobie. At first he was a member of the Spéléo-Club Ragaie de Vedène in the Vaucluse, and explored numerous caves in the Gard, the Ardèche, the Vercors and the Causses. With his companions from the Spéléo-Club of Pont-Saint-Esprit, of which he is one of the founder-members, he was responsible for the discovery and exploration of the Aven des Pèbres, in the Cèze Valley, one of the most beautiful caves in the Gard. In 1985, in the gorges, with François Montel, Françoise Landraud and their friends from Pont-Saint-Esprit, he discovered a continuation of the known part of the Grotte des Deux-Ouvertures, on the walls of which were magnificent engravings of animals and signs dating back to the Solutrean period (it was classed as a historical monument in 1990).

BIRTH OF A TEAM

4. Chauvet Cave is festooned with stalactites and stalagmites of every shape; some are coloured, but they are often very white, with phases of renewal.

It was the new discoveries at the Grotte des Deux-Ouvertures which led Eliette and Christian to meet. As a volunteer correspondent for the region's Prehistoric Antiquities section, Eliette was taking part in a visit to the cave organized by the Direction Régionale des Affaires Culturelles (DRAC). These two enthusiasts got on well and began to carry out explorations together, particularly in the gorges of the Ardèche. Eliette was more familiar with archaeology than with caving techniques, and underwent her apprenticeship in climbing and descending by rope with Christian.

20

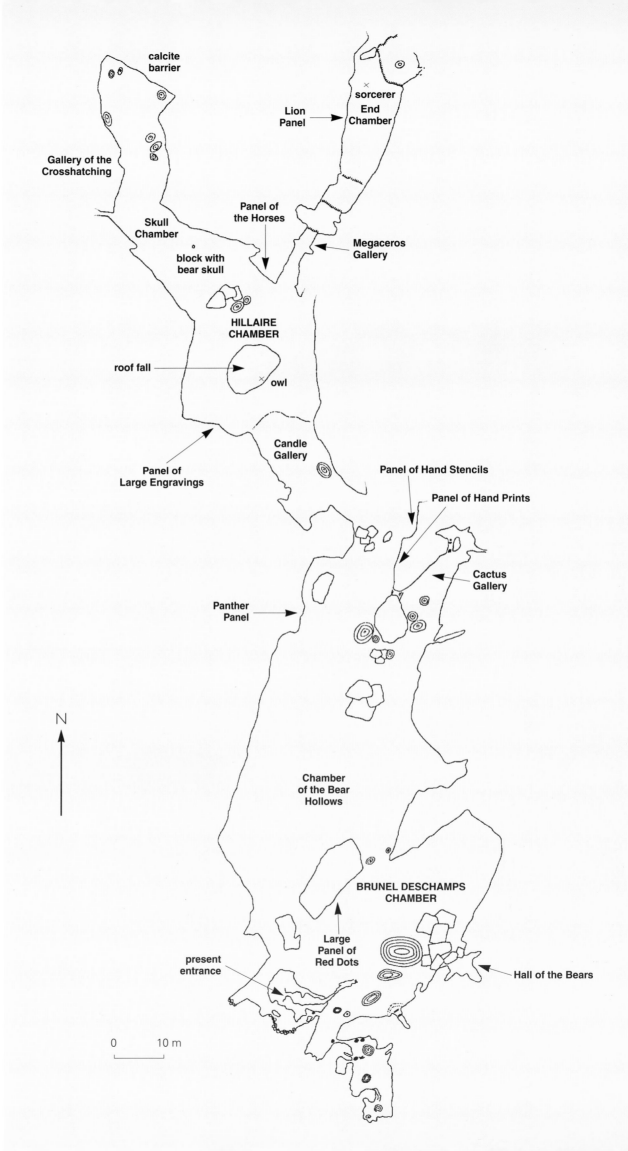

calcite
barrier

Lion
Panel

sorcerer
End
Chamber

Gallery of the
Crosshatching

Skull
Chamber

Panel of
the Horses

Megaceros
Gallery

block with
bear skull

HILLAIRE
CHAMBER

roof fall

owl

Candle
Gallery

Panel of Hand Stencils

Panel of Hand Prints

Panel of
Large Engravings

Cactus
Gallery

Panther
Panel

Chamber
of the Bear
Hollows

BRUNEL DESCHAMPS
CHAMBER

present
entrance

Large
Panel of
Red Dots

Hall of the Bears

N

0   10 m

*5. Plan of Chauvet Cave drawn
up by the discoverers. (Length
500 metres (1700 ft)). Only the
major panels have been
included.*

6. *The Pont d'Arc, a natural arch cut through rock by the Ardèche.*

It was only in 1988, however, that the three of us became a team. The town hall of Saint-Sauveur-de-Cruzières, in the Gard, had asked us, through Robert Brun, discoverer of the Grotte de la Tête-du-Lion, to explore a cave where archaeological remains had already been found. We hoped to find a continuation of the cave. Although our first expedition together was not crowned with success, a bond formed between us. We felt that we had many things in common such as energy and stubborn willpower. We were fired with the same desire to push exploration to the limit and make a contribution to the knowledge of this underground world. From that time onward, we spent all our weekends together, indulging in our passion. We all contributed our experience; each of us knew the location of caves that he or she wanted to explore, so that there was always a destination on the agenda.

In the gorges, as well as in the vicinity of the Saint-André Basin, Berrias and Païolive Wood, a little further west, we explored several hundred caves and swallow-holes. We should stress that, in this total, decorated caves are very much a minority.

EXPLORATION

Exploration is aimed at the discovery and study of the underground world, and this is why all observations concerning geology, crystallography as well as biology and cave faunas, etc., must be carried out. Before any exploration, the first step is to find new caves or a continuation of an already-known cave. The slightest draught coming through scree, or escaping from a burrow or a hole in the ground can be a clue. If air can pass, then it may mean that the cavity communicates with a gallery or perhaps a shaft. To detect it, we sometimes use a smoke-producing coil which we move along the wall or the ground while watching the direction of the smoke. But not all draughts are significant. Some may merely be indicating a simple 'passe-traou', that is, a duct that immediately emerges into the open air on the cliff-face, without leading to the slightest passage. Over the years we have acquired a 'sense of draughts' (humid, dry, turbulent or intermittent). To feel them, Jean-Marie likes to use the back of his hand, while Christian and Eliette prefer to expose their faces to them. But other clues can help us too, such as the morphology of the cave, its dimensions, its geological situation, the resonance of echoes and the temperature and humidity.

At the spot where the draught is strongest, we start clearing away the stones and earth in order to enter the passage. This work can be long and tedious. Once the duct has been cleared, the slimmest or the least tired of us is sent in for a scout around. He or she wriggles through the hole to see if it is worth having the others follow. The first few seconds after entering the passage, when the one who has gone in discovers an unknown gallery, are undoubtedly among the most intense of the exploration. They shine their helmet lamp feverishly in all directions, searching for the slightest sign of a promising continuation, instinctively rejecting the idea that everything could end here.

7. *The Large Panel of Red Dots extends for several metres on the left-hand wall, barely 20 metres (65 ft) from the prehistoric entrance.*

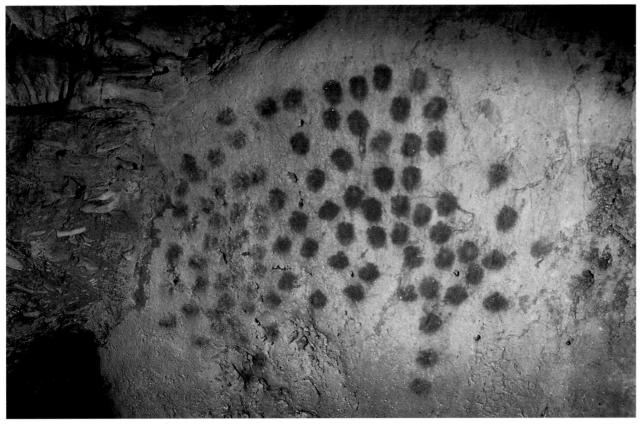

8. *This collection of red dots seems to depict an animal form, perhaps a bison, facing to the right.*

9. To the right of the Large Panel of Red Dots (plate 7), a sign in the shape of a cross surmounts some scarcely visible traces with lateral appendages, which could belong to a sign like the one resembling an insect (plate 16).

If the cave looks interesting, we widen the passage, clearing away material on both sides, and the other two join the first to enter. The exploration can then begin. Being always very respectful of caves, we use acetylene lamps as little as possible, since they leave black trails on ceilings, and if the floor is covered in concretions we walk about in stockinged feet to avoid damaging it. Moreover, in cases where we find archaeological material, we leave absolutely everything in place so that the scientists can study the site exactly as we found it, and sometimes just as prehistoric people left it several thousand years ago. If no protection can be ensured, the objects are collected and deposited in the regional museum of prehistory at Orgnac.

An exploration can last more than ten hours, as was the case at Le Runladou, near Berrias, a few dozen kilometres west of the gorges, which was undoubtedly one of our most tiring. The network had been opened up twenty years ago by the speleological group of Les Vans, which in particular had discovered a big chamber with a roof 30 metres (100 ft) high, partially inundated by a lake and with an impressive echo. Since

10. Two tiny yellow horse heads, facing left, are next to some assemblages of big red dots and stripes.

From left to right and top to bottom:

11. Near the top of a wall with fragile stalactites, an accumulation of ten big red dots.

12. A succinct sketch of the front of a male ibex, recognizable by its long curved horn, facing left (Panther Panel).

13. A big hanging rock is decorated with numerous large dots, some of them covered by a layer of calcite.

14. The Hall of the Bears. A large stag; its technique recalls that of the animals of Pech-Merle and Cougnac in the Lot.

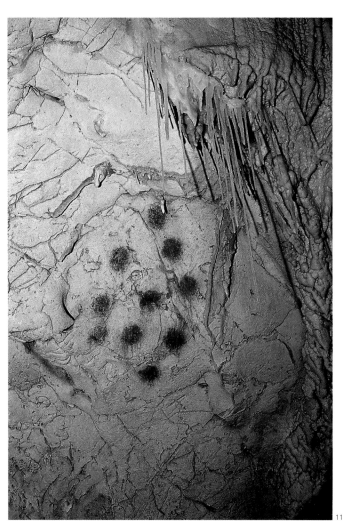

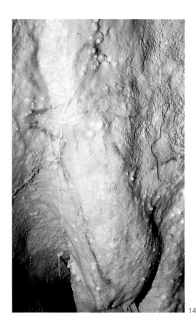

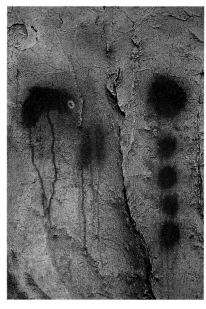

we resumed its exploration in 1989, we have returned many times – only in the summer and during dry weather, because after the least rainfall the network is totally flooded. So far we have been the first people to explore almost 2 kilometres (1 mile) of galleries here. But before reaching the upper levels, where we finally discovered big chambers with beautiful concretions, we first had to cross a narrow passage, obstructed with blocks, by crawling in liquid mud for 10 metres (30 ft), and then equip ourselves for ascents, thus enabling us to climb in stages to a height of more than 40 metres (130 ft). The numerous gallery entrances that we have left untouched mean we can confidently predict several more kilometres to come.

Just above the Runladou network, in 1990, we discovered with some friends a fine archaeological site: the Charaix Cave. It all began with a fox burrow from which a tremendous draught was emerging. We dug a little tunnel there, and after a very long clearance of 25 metres (80 ft) of gallery, we reached the ceiling of a big chamber. We then had to descend a shaft over 30 metres (100 ft) long. There we found an abundance of intact archaeological material: it was a very ancient habitation, arranged in terraces, with supporting walls. Hearths and pottery vessels were preserved. As soon as we detected them, we were careful to walk only on calcified areas, so as not to tread on the sites: one dating from the Bronze Age (1200 BC) and the other from the Copper Age (1800 BC). The cave was very quickly protected by a door, and is now being excavated by archaeologists from the Centre National de la Recherche Scientifique. It will therefore be possible to study this intact site in its entirety.

15. To the left of the yellow horse heads, a little horse head identical to the others was painted, but in red this time. Like the others, it is next to assemblages of dots and lines.

16. Some unusual signs are framed by stalagmite flows: to the right, a branching sign, resembling a big insect; to the left, two butterfly-like signs.

17. The head of an indeterminate animal – bear or feline – partly covered by calcite.

18. An indeterminate animal, probably an ibex; the front of its body has disappeared beneath the calcite.

19. A vertical bear, to the right of the Panther Panel.

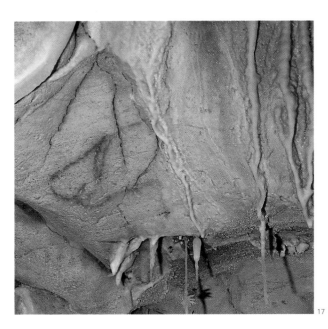

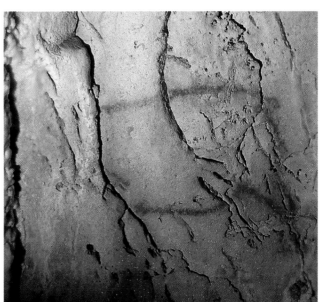

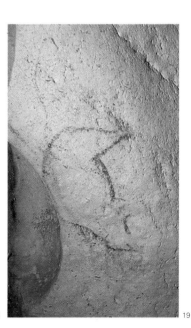

OUR DISCOVERIES IN THE GORGES
OF THE ARDECHE

Building on the work accomplished by Eliette and Bernadette in the course of ten years, we undertook a methodical and in-depth campaign of exploration in the caves on both banks of the gorges of the Ardèche. For three years (1991–93), within the framework of the studies scheduled by the scientific committee of the Ardèche Gorges Reserve, we produced an inventory of archaeological sites and drew up the topography of those which we thought the most interesting (sometimes with the help of our friend Michel Chabaud). In this way numerous unknown sites were listed, monitored and protected. The results of our research were handed over confidentially to the DRAC's Regional Archaeological Service as well as to the Director of the Reserve who is in charge of protection in every domain.

For our investigations in the gorges, we generally proceed as follows: we choose a sector; and there we methodically follow all the cliff bases, all the ledges (those very narrow flat areas that form a path on the flank of the cliff), and we enter every cavity we encounter. Once inside them, we study the floor as well as the walls, and leave no

20. The head and front of a cave-bear, facing left, with shading used inside the head.

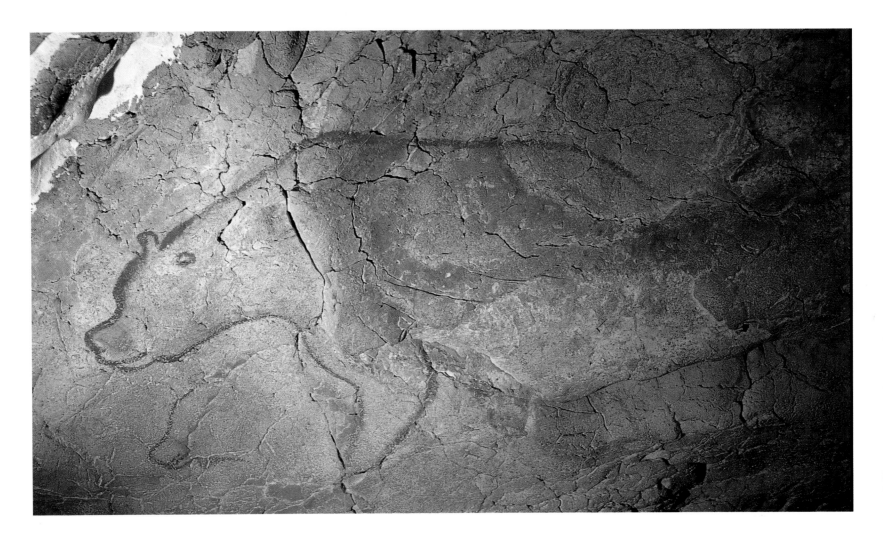

gallery, rock climb or descending shaft unexplored, even in caves that are heavily frequented by other cavers.

THE DECORATED CAVES

Our speleological explorations have led us to discover several decorated caves, as well as archaeological sites. Certain decorated caves, except for the continuation of that of Les Deux-Ouvertures and that of Le Cade, had already been known for a long time. On the other hand, their walls had never really been observed, and we were the first people to notice depictions on them. The first wall art we found together is located in the Grotte du Louoï, in the Ibie Valley (a tributary of the Ardèche), which was a place where phosphate was extracted at the turn of the century. After that discovery we systematically examined the walls of every cave we visited.

In 1991, in a small rock-shelter downstream of the Grotte du Figuier, we found fragments of red paintings. Then, in 1992, in the porch of the Grotte de la Vacheresse – an old sheepfold whose drystone walls still survive, partially closing the entrance – we

21. The Hall of the Bears. This big cave bear, between the heads of two animals of the same species, was produced by using the natural contour for the relief of the front paw. Note the use of shading on the head.

31

found a few prehistoric traces spanning a period from the Palaeolithic to the Bronze Age, as well as paintings and engravings, including a game of hopscotch. In the Caverne des Potiers, which also served as a sheepfold, we noticed numerous finger tracings, some of them covered in calcite, in a small gallery. In the Grotte de la Bergerie, in a huge gallery separated into two parts by a big drystone wall, we found medieval engraved signs. In the rock-shelter of the Combe d'Oulen, in a recess of the cliff, we discovered paintings: an oval, an anthropomorph and a sign.

In 1993, our major discovery (until Chauvet Cave, of course) was that of the Grotte aux Points. In this cave, which takes the form of a large corridor just over 100 metres (330 ft) long, in which there are traces of ancient installations, we first noticed little spots of red ochre, and then found several beautiful depictions, especially the front of a horse, some groups of big red dots, 6–8 centimetres (2–3 in) in diameter, and signs. Dots of this kind were previously unknown in the wall art of the gorges. In 1994, in the Bergerie de Charmasson, we detected numerous finger tracings, covered in calcite; then, in the Grotte du Planchard, a female figure in red ochre beneath the calcite; and finally, in the Aven du Cade, some engravings on the ceiling.

Naturally, none of these caves is comparable with Chauvet Cave, in terms not only of dimensions but also of the abundance of figures, their quality or their state of conservation; but each discovery brings us an additional piece of knowledge about wall art and its distribution in the gorges of the Ardèche. That of Chauvet Cave was an extraordinary shock and the reward for years of work.

THE DISCOVERY OF CHAUVET CAVE

In the course of 1994, our cave explorations continued, not only at weekends but also during all our free time.

The Aven de la Chariette (Berrias-Beaulieu): after a long clearance, we reached an underground river at a depth of less than 115 metres (370 ft). The network comprises 300 metres (980 ft) of gallery like a pipeline, part of it circular in section; a tube, 1.5 metres (5 ft) in diameter, stopped by a siphon both upstream and downstream.

The Charaix Cave: following our discovery of the archaeological site, and working from our topographic plan, we established the connection with the exterior. We unblocked the original entrance porch, which enabled prehistoric people to reach the great chamber, in order to facilitate the archaeologists' work by sparing them the 30-metre (100-ft) shaft.

During the summer we also had outings to the Lozère and, from November onward, we decided to 'visit' or 'revisit' the most sheltered and sunniest parts of the gorges of the Ardèche.

Finally, on 18 December, we had only a few hours in the afternoon at our disposal, and we opted for the Cirque d'Estre, at the entrance of the gorges, which in the cold

22. A small mammoth, facing left, partly erased, painted on a rock hanging down. This utilization of hanging rocks is frequent in Chauvet Cave.

weather is very pleasant in full sunlight. Of course we knew the numerous sheepfolds, tiers of which are located in these cliffs; but we decided to see the caves that we had not bothered with so far, since they had seemed to be of secondary interest.

We had explored this sector several times with our friend Erwin Tscherter, a speleologist and archaeologist who has been working in this region for more than thirty years, without suspecting for a single instant the treasure that lay beneath our feet.

A PATH ALONG THE CLIFF

On 18 December, we reached the gorges around three o'clock in the afternoon. It was a fine and cold winter Sunday. The cliff of the Cirque d'Estre overhangs the ancient bed of the Ardèche which now flows a few hundred metres further away. Where the slope becomes more gentle, it is covered by evergreen oaks, heath and boxtrees which have invaded natural terraces. We took an ancient mule path which, halfway up, came out onto a narrow ledge, bathed in sunlight – a providential belvedere from which we could admire that marvellous site of the Pont d'Arc. At our feet there stretched vineyards and the tourist road through the gorges. Then we advanced into denser vegetation and arrived at the entrance of a little cavity. Located two metres above the ground, in the white cliff mingled with grey and ochre, it measured about 80 centimetres (30 in) high and 30 centimetres (10 in) wide. Once we had passed this narrow opening, we found ourselves in a small, sloping vestibule, several metres long, pierced by numerous passages cut by the waters. The ceiling was low, and we could only just stand up. It was slightly less cold in there than outside, and the atmosphere was dry.

At the end, the ceiling became rounded. The slope of the floor led us towards what could have been the continuation of the gallery at a spot where a slight draught was perceptible. Lying on the floor, head downward, we took it in turns to pull out stones. We continued to feel the draught. But we were worried that the rock and the earth were too dry, and feared we were in a simple 'passe-traou'. As always, we were heading for the unknown, advancing centimetre by centimetre, without knowing what the next stage would bring – perhaps nothing. The duct descended vertically, made a turn, then ascended again. After about 3 metres (10 ft) it opened out. With head first, and arms outstretched in front of her, Eliette wriggled into the clayey narrowness, using the light from her helmet lamp. It was six thirty in the evening. Triumphant, she could see the floor 10 metres (30 ft) below her: so there was a continuation! In our impatience, we joined her. To measure the resonance of the echo, we shouted. The noise carried far, and seemed to get lost in the immensity of the cave. As sometimes happens, we were certainly above a big gallery. We were filled with enthusiasm, feeling that an amazing 'première' was in store for us. But in order to descend, a ladder was needed.

We therefore had to return to the van, parked at the foot of the cliff, to get the necessary equipment. But once we were down, we suddenly felt very tired. It was already

23. The Panther Panel. Above the big animal (hyena or bear), one can just make out the simple outline of a large bear, facing left.

dark, the air was even colder than in the early afternoon, and we did not feel strong enough to go all the way back to the cavity. So we decided to go home and return the following weekend – Christmas weekend. However, after some hesitation, the fear of someone else having the 'première' before us led us to climb back up.

FIRST STEPS IN AN IMMENSE GALLERY

After crawling through the narrow passage a second time, we arrived at the edge of the shaft, unrolled our ladder and, one after the other, climbed down into the profound darkness of the cave. In our impatience, the descent seemed endless, especially as we could not see the walls. Jean-Marie was first to reach the floor. It felt good, the pleasant odour of wet clay filling our nostrils. Our hearts were thumping: a magnificent cave network was opening up before us. The gallery that the beams from our helmet lamps were lighting so feebly was immense. We were impressed by its dimensions, which were very rare in the gorges: about 15 metres (50 ft) high, surely more in places, and almost fifty in length. The silence was total. We were now completely cut off from the world, immersed in that mineral universe that we love so much. By the light of our lamps we were fascinated to discover some monumental columns of white calcite to our right. Some took the form of gigantic jellyfish, others were like carved mother-of-pearl pillars. Draperies hung from the ceiling, the crystals shining with a thousand fires. Everything was too beautiful, the spectacle was unreal.

We moved in single file through the darkness, each of us trying to follow the foot-prints of the one in front, so as to leave only one track and not damage the floor of the cave. The floor was covered by a sparkling film of white calcite, crossed by thousands of calcified wavelets. It was unusually flat and regular. On the left, two deep subsidences plunged into the earth – craters several metres in diameter. Without exploring the end of this first chamber, we continued our journey towards the left, attracted by great flows of mother-of-pearl calcite of exceptional whiteness marking the entrance of a second gallery. We were filled with wonder by a white disc, as translucent as porcelain, that stood out on the wall.

A new chamber, far larger than the preceding one, now met our gaze. It seemed to stretch for dozens and dozens of metres. Our lamps did not enable us to see the end, and we could scarcely see the walls. Darkness dominated all around us. Our excitement grew, since caves this large were totally unknown in the gorges. We had already seen beautiful chambers with concretions, but very few of such size. In our euphoria we gazed feverishly in all directions, trying to note as many details as possible. It was at this moment that we discovered multitudes of bear bones and teeth strewn over the floor, which was calcified here and there. Advancing slowly, we redoubled our precautions to avoid crushing them. All around us were dozens of depressions dug into the earth, as if the ground had been bombed. We recognized them as the 'nests' in which

24. Two butterfly-like signs, of different sizes, and two vertical lines take up the whole of the lower part of this hanging rock.

36

THE PANEL OF
HAND PRINTS

25. *The Panel of Hand Prints*
with, top left, the end of the line
of rhinoceroses, and, in the
centre at the bottom, a
rhinoceros facing right with an
enormous horn.

bears must have hibernated. A strange lunar landscape. Magnificent, translucent, fistulous stalactites hung from the ceiling like angels' hair. At the end of the chamber there rose a calcite barrier, as pure as snow.

TRACES OF RED OCHRE

26. The Panel of Hand Prints. Below an animal facing right and in front of the head of another feline, several positive hands and a semi-circle of little dots have been drawn in red paint.

We then took a narrower gallery on our right, still in single file by the light of our head-lamps, and stepped over a rock covered by a shining film of calcite. Suddenly, as Eliette's gaze swept the wall, she gave a cry: in the beam of her lamp she had just made out two lines of red ochre, a few centimetres long. We joined her with beating hearts. On turning round, we immediately spotted the drawing of a little red mammoth on a rocky spur hanging down from the ceiling. We were overwhelmed. Henceforth our

plate 22

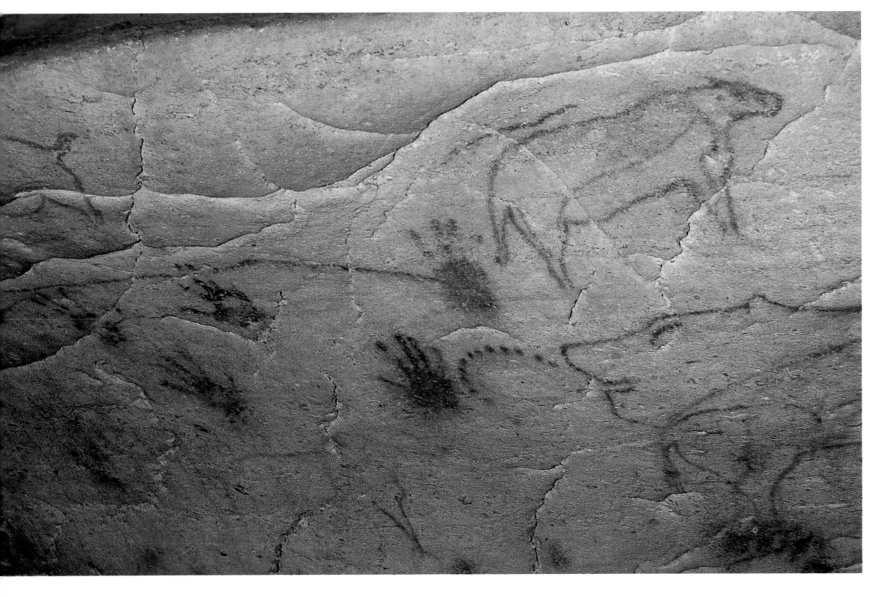

40

view of the cave would never be the same. Prehistoric people had been here before us. Bearing in mind its size, we were surely going to discover more figures in it.

In this very colourful gallery, the calcite is mingled with orange. We were dazzled by a myriad crystals, white 'cacti' had grown on the floor and colonnades formed a barrier of very pure concretions. Vigilant now, we feverishly scanned the walls with our headlamps. Suddenly, on the left, in the middle of a white wall, a big red bear over a metre high rose up before us. Transfixed, we stayed for a moment to admire it. Growing increasingly excited, we moved forward slowly, always careful about where we set our feet, determined to stick to the prints of the person ahead and eager to examine the walls. Having reached a cul-de-sac, we saw numerous incised lines and, on the floor, some bones and a bear skull. We had to retrace our steps, following our footprints back to the second chamber where we had branched off; this time we returned to the main gallery.

DEPICTIONS OF A KIND UNKNOWN IN THE ARDECHE

The concretions were becoming more and more beautiful, and taking on copper colours. Like lengths of tissue escaping from the rock, delicate draperies hung down from the ceiling. The floor had become an intense orange, with little calcite ridges winding and sparkling across it. To the right, we found more paintings in red ochre: a
plates 16,24 complex sign, and then what seemed to us to be a big butterfly or a bird of prey with outspread wings, a shape that we found again to the left on an overhang. In a few minutes our discoveries multiplied. A little further, on the white rock, there appeared
plate 25 the front of an immense red rhinoceros, endowed with an impressive curved horn. This was a real shock, because no depiction of a rhinoceros had ever been seen in the Ardèche caves.

On bending down, we discovered a mammoth, then a bear or lion (a semicircle
plate 26 of little dots seemed to emerge from its muzzle like drops of blood), and other rhinoceroses. To the right, we could make out three lion heads. We saw hands, several of them positive and one negative, which were also totally unknown in the region. Following this great panel painted in red ochre, there were dozens of big red dots; a
plate 28 little further on, two hand stencils and some dots. In total, a frieze of 10 metres (30 ft) in length, in front of which we remained for a long time, sitting on our heels and gazing in contemplation. As we always do, we kept our distance and made no attempt to approach the painted wall in order to preserve any prints that the prehistoric people might have left at its foot, as well as any possible bowls or pellets of red ochre.

During those moments there were only shouts and exclamations; the emotion that gripped us made us incapable of uttering a single word. Alone in that vastness, lit by the feeble beam of our lamps, we were seized by a strange feeling. Everything was so beautiful, so fresh, almost too much so. Time was abolished, as if the tens of thousands of years that separated us from the producers of these paintings no longer existed. It seemed as if they had just created these masterpieces. Suddenly we felt like intruders. Deeply impressed, we were weighed down by the feeling that we were not alone; the artists' souls and spirits surrounded us. We thought we could feel their presence; we were disturbing them.

Christian and Jean-Marie moved forward and crossed a low passage, while Eliette remained totally absorbed by the spectacle of the red frieze. We found ourselves in a huge gallery and could not make out its far end. The power of our lights was diminishing. Since we had not yet memorized the cave's topography, we thought it prudent to retrace our steps. We did not wish to risk getting lost. Following our footprints, we crossed the second chamber again. The floor was made up of millions of sharp calcite crystals. On our right, two disconcerting apparitions left us absolutely stunned once more: on the light rock, drawn in red ochre, were two superb animals with spotted bodies, which seemed to us to be a hyena and a panther, accompanied by other drawings of an ibex and a bear. Once again, the two former motifs had never been seen in the gorges of the Ardèche.

plate 23
plate 12

We reached the concretions that separate the two great chambers. Knowing that we were now close to the exit shaft, we took the time to look all around us before climbing

27. The Panel of Hand Prints. On the left of this big panel, four rhinoceroses follow each other, well framed on a strip of rock. The first, more schematic than the rest, has its ears drawn as double semi-circles.

back up. On the floor, near the passage between the two chambers, we saw a fine ibex skull covered with calcite and very well preserved – the two horns had lost their points, but the jaw was intact. Then we saw a bear skull, half sunk into the clay. We now discovered that the walls of the first chamber were covered with numerous depictions which stood out one by one as our lamps caught them. To our left, at the end, there appeared numerous dots and a beautiful deer painted in red ochre. Some dots are high up, and the prehistoric people must have climbed onto blocks of calcite to make them. This immediately evoked the Grotte des Points, our discovery of the previous year. Then, opposite, we lit up a group of closely packed dots: it was an animal made up entirely of these same big red spots. To judge by its posture, it seems to be a bison or a rhinoceros, and this beautiful composition looks very modern.

At this spot, an earth tremor had brought some great columns crashing to the floor, which was strewn with blocks of calcite. If one continues towards a wall right at the end of the chamber, one discovers in a crevice a little panel made up of dots and a small red mammoth, in a style just like those in the cave of Oulen. Two tiny and unusual horse heads in yellow ochre attracted our attention. Other dots are covered with calcite. Being short of lighting, we reemerged, completely stunned, and reblocked the narrow passage with lots of stones, so that nobody could enter the cave and cause

28. The Panel of Hand Stencils with several groups of dots and, to the right, a black horse under the calcite.

irreparable damage. We were almost relieved to be back in the chilly air of the gorges.

This first visit had lasted only an hour, but we were in a state of shock because of our discovery – both moved and, in a way, crushed by the weight of such a responsibility. We were far from having seen everything the cave contains (we had not even explored half of it), but already we felt that this was an extraordinary ensemble: with the extent and beauty of the chambers, the numerous bear bones and the abundance of those magnificent prehistoric paintings, including several depictions hitherto unknown in the region, all in a remarkable state of preservation. Exhausted by so many emotions, we went to eat at Eliette's, where we joined Carole, her twenty-two-year-old daughter. The disjointed and emotion-filled account we gave her had unexpected consequences: Carole doubted the truthfulness of our tale and asked to see for herself. After a quarter of an hour's negotiation, we finally gave in.

THE PANEL OF THE HORSES

Around nine o'clock at night, we overcame our fatigue and set off again. Once more we climbed up; we reopened the duct, and for the second time we went through the galleries, lit now by powerful torches which we had taken the precaution of bringing along. The dimensions and shimmering colours of the concretions could now be seen more distinctly. It was like a new discovery, we were amazed all over again. For

29. A horse and other engravings. The difference in colour between the stomach and the breast of the horses is marked by a line in the shape of a flattened 'M'. Note a broad undulating trail on the upper part of the body. This horse was engraved on top of numerous ancient clawmarks.

example, in the first chamber, on a wall to the left, we noticed a composition of red dots, washed out by the humidity and covered by a film of calcite; it was 4–5 metres plate 7 (13–16 ft) long, but had escaped our attention before. During our first visit, we were so busy discovering the mineral forms and watching where we stepped that we had not noticed all the walls, which in any case were very remote – the cave was vast. Following our earlier footprints exactly, we arrived in front of the big red rhinoceros frieze. Eliette and Carole stayed there a few moments, gazing at it in wonder.

Christian and Jean-Marie continued into the gallery, of which we had had only a fleeting glimpse a few hours earlier; it was decorated with white, yellow and orange concretions, in often intense shades. We took the time to play our lights over this extravagant decor. Bear bones were strewn over the orange floor. Hearths made of big pieces of charcoal, thousands of years old, looked as if they had been extinguished the day before. On the walls, marks where torches had been wiped bore witness to the passage of prehistoric people, and multitudes of clawmarks showed the presence of bears. Which came here first? We were not certain we would find more paintings, but everything was beautiful in this gallery: the astonishing flows of red calcite, a waterfall of terraced hollows filled with clear water, eccentric and fistulous stalactites as pure as crystal, a stalagmite in the shape of a white candle (with a triangular cross-section – a rarity for the experienced caver). We revelled in this magnificent spectacle.

We now entered a very large chamber in the centre of which was an immense crater, 10 metres (30 ft) in diameter. We passed to its right. Here, the floor was covered with brown earth. On an overhang, just above this subsidence, we discovered the first

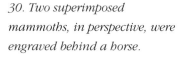

30. Two superimposed mammoths, in perspective, were engraved behind a horse.

46

31. Above a ceiling with a
beautiful calcite drapery, a
bear facing left seems to be
following an indeterminate
animal, of which only the line
of the back is visible.

plate 35

plate 45

plate 53
plate 55
plate 61
plate 59

plate 64

32. Horse facing left, engraved on an overhang close to that where the owl is located. Note the two lines at the shoulder and the duckbill muzzle.

33. An owl, seen from the front, on an overhang. This is the only depiction of this creature known in Palaeolithic art.

engravings, their white incisions still standing out clearly from the light-coloured stone: a horse and, next to it, an owl – a depiction quite unique in Palaeolithic art – then a strange shape that looked like a wild goose or a duck. If there was further need, here was proof of the antiquity of the figures, since they now overhung a hole some 5–6 metres (16–20 ft) deep. But in fact we had not doubted for a moment that we were in the presence of authentic Palaeolithic works. There were bear prints in the earth, and we also saw a complete skeleton, intact and still articulated.

We moved on; a torch lit up the end of the chamber, and there was a moment of ecstasy. An extraordinary black frieze appeared: with magnificent horses; aurochs with beautiful S-shaped horns – recalling those of the Ebbou Cave; rhinoceroses – two of them facing each other in a confrontation or an amorous joust; an astonishing little stylized bison; a bear. To the right of an apse containing three calm, pensive horse heads, there were lions, one of which was very strange and seemed a bit of a failure; the one below, on the other hand, was admirable, its eye surmounted by an eyebrow, its muzzle surrounded by whiskers, and a few red signs on its neck. But there were also stags, ibex, and a magnificent bison whose multiple legs evoked a running movement. In the excitement of discovery, we tried to take everything in with one look. Over more than 10 metres (30 ft), animals drawn in charcoal form a harmonious composition that uses the wall's volumes, its crevices, its angles, producing illusions of relief and perspective. Natural flows of ochre colour the supporting rock.

48

The horses are splendid, depicted with a remarkable realism and sense of detail: the pupils, nostrils and half-open muzzles are breathtakingly lifelike. The outline of the lowest one has been scraped to make it clearer. Shading gives an impression of volume. The aesthetic mastery of these artists is exceptional, and we could hardly believe our eyes. The cave ranks with the masterpieces of world Palaeolithic art, as beautiful as Altamira or Lascaux. Jean-Marie, who a few moments before had pointed out that we had not yet found any horses, was stammering. Christian was uttering exclamations of amazement. When Eliette and Carole rushed over, they overflowed with joy and emotion in their turn, trying to release the tension we were all feeling. These were minutes of indescribable madness. But again our wonder was mingled with a kind of anxiety. We almost had the feeling that we were desecrating a sanctuary that had remained hidden for thousands of years. Since the Palaeolithic people had left we were the first to enter these protected places.

We followed the direction the animals were looking in, which seemed to be an invitation to continue towards the left. In a recess behind this great frieze, we found engravings of ibex and mammoths which we did not go near: at the foot of this wall, the soft clay might have preserved the footprints of the Palaeolithic people. A little further on we were deeply impressed by what we discovered. In the middle of the chamber, on a block of grey stone of regular shape that had fallen from the ceiling, the skull of a bear was placed as if on an altar. The animal's fangs projected beyond it into the air. On the top of the stone there were still pieces of charcoal, the remains of a fireplace. All around, on the floor, there were more than thirty bear skulls; now covered in a frosting of amber-coloured calcite, they were purposely set out on the earth. There were no traces of skeletons. This intentional arrangement troubled us because of its solemn peculiarity. A few metres away, on the left, some engravings and black paintings had been drawn on overhangs – mammoths, a reindeer, and an aurochs.

plate 40

We pressed on towards a narrower gallery, its walls incised by bear claws, and its floor covered with numerous bones. Some parts of the walls were smooth where the bears must have rubbed against them. The ceiling was low and we advanced, bent over, towards the end of this corridor, closed by a barrier of calcite that blazed with colour. Stalagmites and stalactites had grown everywhere, and the floor was covered by a thick carpet of copper-coloured concretions. At the end, on a yellow ceiling, a horse was engraved and, to the left, there was a geometric sign in the form of cross-hatching that intrigued us. We had reached the end of the cave. But this gallery, now blocked by concretion flows, must have continued previously.

On returning to the third chamber, and passing round the opposite side of the crater, our lamps lit up another beautiful engraved frieze: with an elegant moving horse – its left foreleg raised and its flank marked by an undulating incision – deer, mammoths, a bear and finger markings. On the floor, which was heavily calcified in places, next to a bear skull on which a stalagmite had grown, we were moved to discover some human footprints. Animal tracks as well as a human hand were also imprinted on the

34. *A bear skull was placed on the edge of a block fallen from the ceiling. Its spectacular appearance has already given rise to numerous risky speculations about the relationship between people and bears in this cave.*

35. *The bears in the course of their visits left numerous traces on the soft earth, like this characteristic pawprint.*

36. *This ibex skull, with its horns preserved, was covered by a layer of calcite.*

37. *A bear skull partly coated with calcite.*

38. *The floors are strewn with cave-bear bones. In the centre two skulls surrounded by various bones can be seen.*

earth, as if frozen in the calcite and miraculously preserved for thousands of years. We rapidly returned towards the shaft. Feeling weighed down with such strong emotions, we wanted to leave. We had been there for almost three hours. The discoveries, each one more gripping than the last, had followed in quick succession at a frantic pace. On leaving, we noticed many more bear bones, some of them even stuck into the ground plate 38 at the foot of the walls.

Towards midnight we finally emerged, taking the greatest care to block up the narrow entrance passage. We descended in silence, preoccupied by the almost fantastic images we had just been contemplating now wrenched from the darkness and the oblivion in which they had remained for thousands of years. Once back home, we broke open the champagne to celebrate this extraordinary discovery. We knew that we had just found a major sanctuary of Palaeolithic art, together with an archaeological site of exceptional richness. We had each just experienced the greatest day in our entire careers as speleologists.

We felt immense joy, but also knew that we now shouldered a very heavy burden of responsibility. This intact site, so exceptional not only from the speleological but also the crystallographic and archaeological point of view, must be protected at all costs. We must restore it to the world just as we found it, avoiding the slightest blemish from the very outset of the visits that would rapidly ensue from experts, authorities, scientists etc. During the following week we each resumed our professional activities, while devising a plan for protecting the floor. At last we found a solution.

THE LION PANEL

On the following Saturday, 24 December, we returned to the cave. To protect the floor we had decided to install a plastic strip throughout our circuit. We would select a single path, and that would become the only possible route for all future investigations. We also equipped ourselves with good lamps. Christian brought a video camera, and Jean-Marie his photographic gear. We wanted to immortalize these marvels. Three caving friends of ours, Daniel André, Michel Chabaud and Jean-Louis Payan, accompanied us that day; we were keen to have them share in our discovery. At nine o'clock in the morning we all met at a car park in Vallon-Pont-d'Arc where they left their cars. A whole group of cars at the foot of the cliff would risk attracting attention. We wanted to look like simple ramblers, but our mountain rucksacks contained caving gear. In fact, it was not long before we came across some hunters who were organizing a beat in search of wild boar.

The sunshine was dazzling, and a light white frost still covered the carpets of moss. We climbed in silence through the woods and moorland. This time, with discretion always our concern, we took a different path that was particularly steep. We stopped for a few moments in the porch of the Grotte de la Vacheresse, very close to our

39. A hanging rock with reindeer and mammoths in the Skull Chamber.

52

40. *Two mammoths face to face on a hanging rock in the Skull Chamber.*

destination, where we had our morning's picnic: as usual, sausage and cheese, washed down with wine from Eliette's vines. We were to spend several hours in the cave, and there was no question of eating inside it, where the crumbs could cause a proliferation of bacteria and moulds. Once again we found ourselves in the little cavity, where, out of sight, we donned our overalls. It took us half an hour's effort to clear away the stones and earth with which we had reblocked the narrow passage.

Once we were down, our friends marvelled at what they were discovering in their turn, while Jean-Marie moved forward, unrolling the plastic sheet, about 50 centimetres (20 in) wide, over our footprints of 18 December. We passed through the galleries, delighted by our companions' excitement, and happy to be back in this extraordinary place. Having reached the great Panel of the Horses, we noticed in the shadows to the right a recess where a rhinoceros, with a curious ventral stripe, was drawn opposite a megaceros (a kind of giant deer). As we approached, we discovered a still unexplored   plate 68 gallery, which had only been glimpsed the first time. The feverish excitement and enthusiasm for a 'première' gripped us once again. We advanced slowly, unrolling the black plastic beneath our feet. We only had 5 metres (15 ft) of it left, but this was enough to make us realize that this gallery was deep. It followed a gentle slope interrupted at times by abrupt steps.

We decided to continue without the plastic, carefully walking on the clay which was very slippery in this part of the cave, and trying to find the hardest areas of the

41. On a hanging rock a black animal facing to the left and some indeterminate red traces were largely obliterated by later scraping.

42. On the other side of the Panel of the Horses, facing the Skull Chamber, several ibex were engraved. One of them is marked with a long line on its body.

floor. We often almost fell. The entire lengths of the walls were incised with engravings and bear clawmarks. The gallery opened out. More depictions followed in succession, and we were filled with wonder at discovering so many more. There were engravings of animals and stylized vulvas (one of which seemed to have a phallus drawn on it); plates 70,73 then a group of beautiful black figures appeared: horses, mostly facing the exit, some plate 72 megaceroses, and a little rhinoceros with an engraved and painted ventral strip drawn inside another bigger one which was looking downwards. On the floor there were abundant hearths, which must have been used for lighting by the artists. We noticed a flint, perhaps one of the tools used for the engravings.

plate 78 Then, to the left, a depiction with shading in red ochre, doubtless a lion head, seemed to have been gashed by bear claws, showing therefore that the bears passed through here after the people. On the right, there was an engraved sign in the form of a roof (like the one in the Grotte aux Points) and numerous finger tracings. A few steps further on, the perfect outline of a horse was drawn, its body filled with flat black colouring. Lower down, a big lion made up of three superimposed lines (a red line plate 79 sandwiched between two black ones) was facing the back of the gallery; below it, a magnificent mammoth was engraved. We had difficulty controlling our breathing, and our hearts were beating fast, as we slowly moved onward. The slope became steeper, and blocks of stone formed a kind of crude staircase. We were reaching the end of the gallery, which was obstructed by concretions. Some pillars of orange calcite had been decorated with red dots.

Suddenly our lamps lit up a monumental black frieze that covered 10 metres (30 ft) of the left-hand wall. It took our breath away as, silently, we played our torches over its panels. There was a burst of shouts of joy and tears. We felt gripped by madness and dizziness. The animals were innumerable: a dozen lions or lionesses (they had no manes), rhinoceroses, bison, mammoths, a reindeer, most of them facing the exit. A curious little mammoth drew our attention, it was almost a chimaera. A magnificent bison – with a curly mane, its horns drawn full face but its head in profile and with its muzzle half-open – was covered with bear clawmarks. And to the right, on an over-hang, our friend Daniel noticed a figure with a bison's head and a human body which seemed to us to be a sorcerer supervising this immense frieze. Under the black figures one can make out ancient red lines that indicate the existence of earlier paintings.

plate 81

plate 93

plate 87

Once again we were filled with admiration at the refinement of the composition. One of the lions seemed to dominate the pride with its penetrating gaze; its head was drawn with darker lines. With theatrical effect, a horse had been placed at the back of a niche and some bison heads were superimposed like hunting trophies. A rhinoceros was endowed with multiple horns that suggested movement. The relief of the rock had

43. This mammoth, with its trunk well depicted, seems to have been endowed with three tusks.

44. Front view of the bear skull which was placed on the edge of a block fallen from the ceiling.

THE PANEL OF
THE HORSES

45. *This great ensemble shows the Panel of the Horses and the facing rhinoceroses, on the left, followed by some horse heads and two felines, then a central niche with the seven-legged bison, the vertical animal and the cow, on its right-hand wall. To the right is the Reindeer Panel. A certain composition, in relation to the niche with animals of different species, seems to have been sought in the layout.*

46. Christian Hillaire crouching in front of the Panel of the Horses.

been used masterfully: the head of a little bison had been drawn full face on a small projection of the wall, whereas its body was in profile, slightly recessed, as if the animal had turned to look at us. We were so filled with awe that we almost forgot to continue our exploration. Determined not to tread on virgin surfaces or risk trampling the bear bones that stretched away to our right, we headed to the left. But we saw on the floor what seemed to be ibex prints, so we decided against continuing, because the earth was covered with animal tracks. Having returned to the frieze, we opened the bottle of champagne that Daniel had had the foresight to bring, and daydreamed as we gazed at this masterpiece. We were happy to be in the company of our friends on the occasion of this new discovery, one of the cave's major panels.

On returning to the great Panel of the Horses, we were admiring it again, quite enthralled, when we noticed some more prints at the foot of a wall: two hands imprinted in a narrow strip of clay. The palms were quite visible, pressed deeper than the lightly marked fingers. Perhaps these were the prints of one of the artists, and the sight of these fragile traces, preserved after so many centuries, was overwhelming. As we returned to the exit, in the first chamber, to our left, we climbed over more fallen blocks that have accumulated on the floor. Behind them, in a recess, there appeared a deer drawn in red. On all fours we reached the entrance of a narrow orange-coloured plate 14

62

47. Jean-Marie Chauvet in front of the Panel of the Horses.

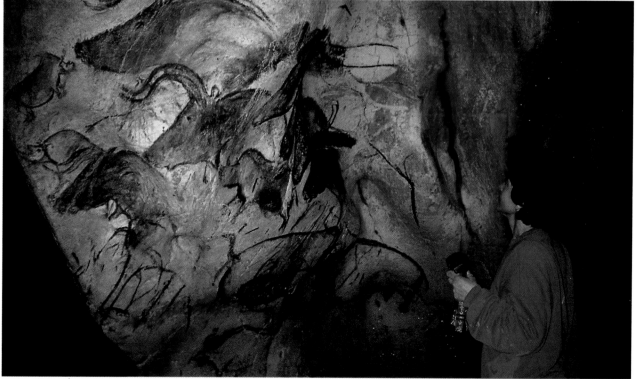

48. Eliette Brunel Deschamps in front of the Panel of the Horses.

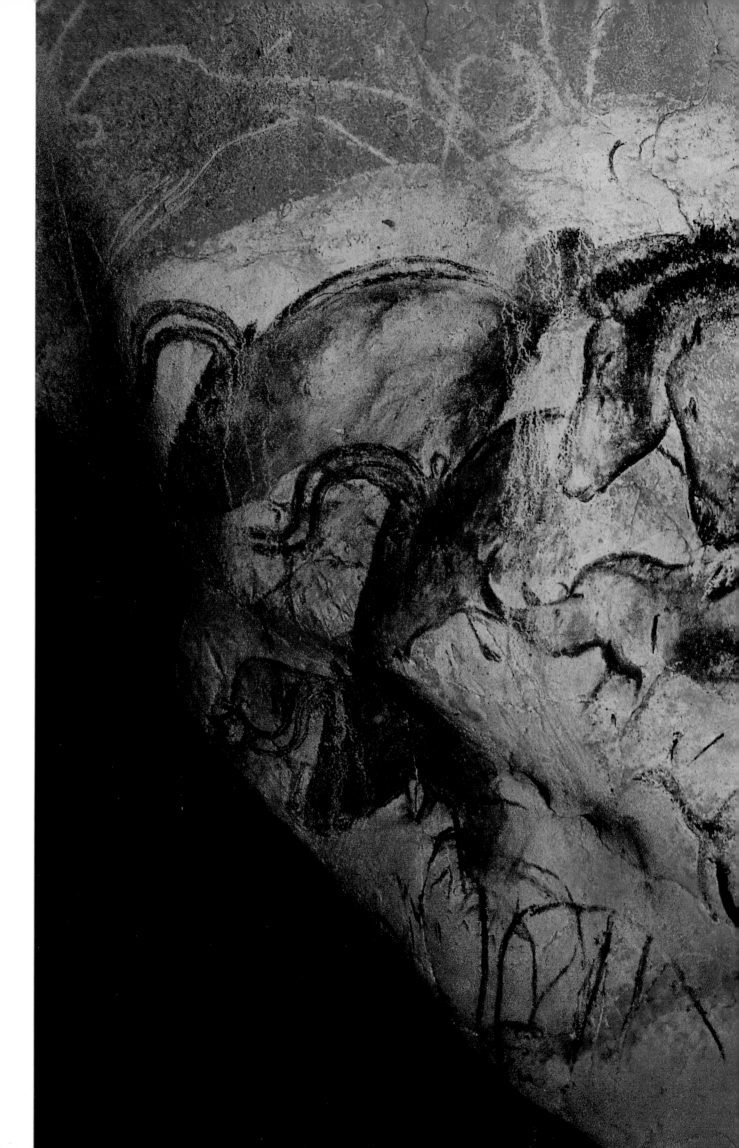

49. *The whole of the Panel of the Horses.*

vestibule, barely more than a metre high. At the back of this tiny cavity, protected by a kind of curtain of golden concretions, was a succession of three magnificent red bears. plate 21 We did not go further forward, because here too the floor was covered with a multitude of bones. This was to be our last discovery. We had lost all track of time. Almost seven hours had already passed since we had come through the narrow passage. We were starving, and it was time to leave.

We got changed inside the entrance vestibule and came down again, like peaceful hikers. But we had lumps in our throats from the emotion. We all decided to give the cave Jean-Marie's name, because it was he who had led us there. Our friends left us, tears in their eyes, still wondering if it was all a dream. Around six o'clock we went our separate ways, each returning to his or her family to celebrate Christmas. The following day was also devoted to family festivities. But the cave's images never left our thoughts.

THE CAVE'S MORPHOLOGY

We had now explored all the accessible parts of Chauvet Cave, which extends for 500 metres (1700 ft) in a single level. It is decorated with magnificent crystallizations and concretions, white in the first chambers, then astonishingly and brilliantly coloured beyond. There is a succession of four chambers of impressive dimensions, in which there are numerous painted or engraved figures. Lateral galleries and vestibules are also decorated. The height of the ceilings varies between 15 metres (50 ft) and 30 metres (100 ft). The first two chambers are decorated with drawings done in red ochre; in the third, first there are engravings and then the black figures which cover the end of the cave. As one walks away from the entrance shaft, in the first chamber, where the concretions are predominantly white, one first sees on the left a frieze of red dots, stretching for more than 10 metres (30 ft); then, at the end, three red panels: the animal made up of dots, the ensemble with the two yellow horse heads, and the red deer accompanied by dots. To the right, behind the chaotic accumulation of blocks, lies the Hall of the Bears.

When one passes into the second chamber with the bear hollows (which measures almost 70 metres (230 ft) by 40 metres (130 ft)), on the left one finds the hyena and the panther; then, to the right, some red signs. At the end, on the right, is the entrance to the Cactus Gallery, over 20 metres (65 ft) long, in which we found the first lines drawn in red ochre. On the left of the chamber is a narrowing where the frieze of the rhinoceroses appears. This is followed by the Candle Gallery, around 30 metres (100 ft) long, with red concretions of red and orange. In the centre of the third chamber is an immense subsidence, above which, on the right, hang engraved animal figures, including the owl. On the left there is an engraved panel over 10 metres (30 ft) long. At the end of the chamber is the Panel of the Horses. To its right, is the Megaceros Gallery and further on is the End Chamber, about 50 metres (165 ft) in length, with a change in

50. The four aurochs and three rhinoceroses on the left of the Panel of the Horses.

66

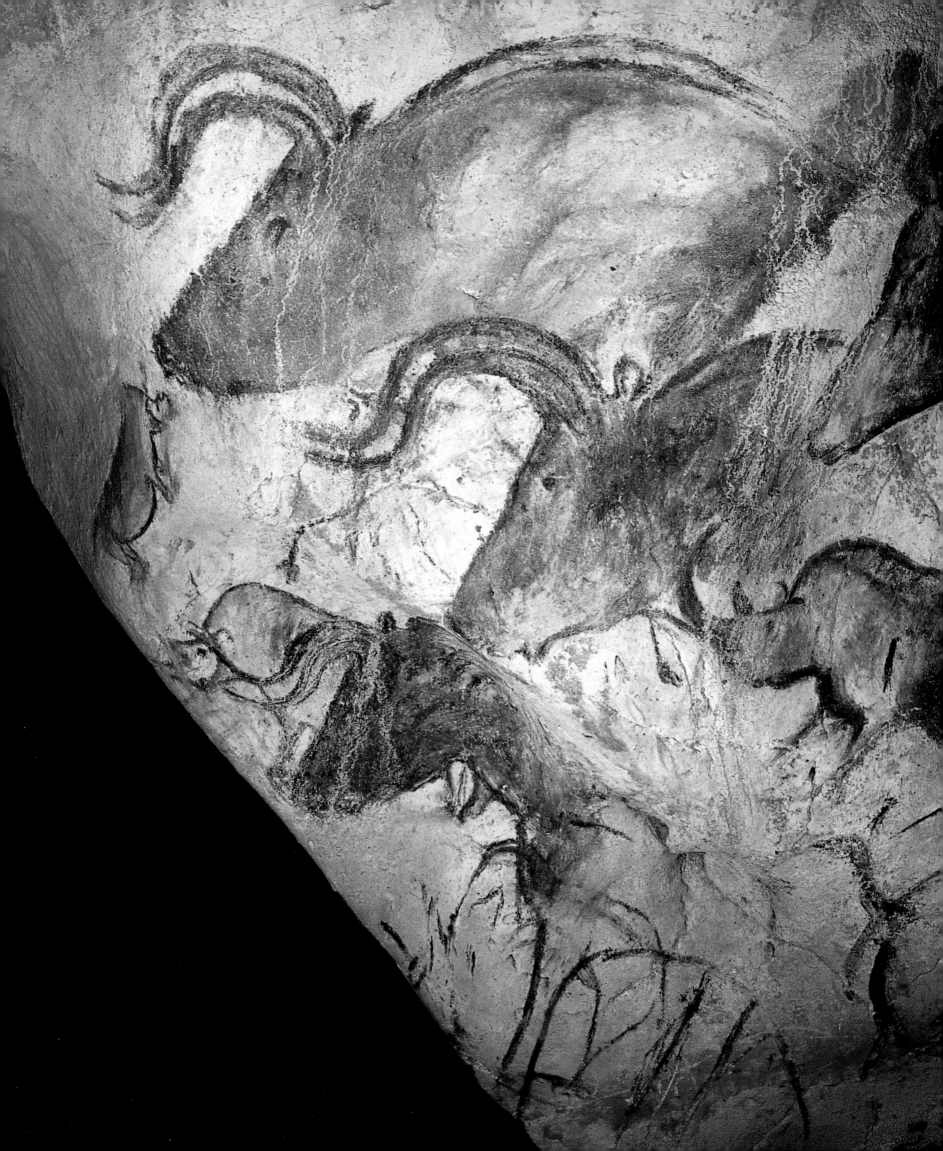

51. The four horses in perspective.

elevation of about 10 metres (30 ft). By following the direction in which the horses are looking, one reaches the Skull Chamber, 20 metres (65 ft) long, and, on the left at the end, the little Gallery of the Crosshatching, blocked off by calcite.

It is a veritable museum. Wherever one looks, one is gripped by the beauty of the mineral forms or the drawn figures. Almost all the drawings are in a remarkable state of preservation. But the interest of this cave is not merely artistic; it is also an exceptional archaeological site. Through its richness, it will enable scholars to make advances in scientific knowledge in numerous fields. Undoubtedly, several decades will be necessary to make a complete study, which will have to be gradual in order to avoid any damage. The first phase will be a study of the cave's climatology to establish its humidity, temperature and ventilation. That will permit useful measures to be taken to protect it from any abrupt modifications of the equilibrium that has made the preservation of its riches possible. In terms of geology and speleology, scientists will wish to determine this cave's evolution, the origin of its creation and its stages of development. The orientation of the crystallizations will inform them about the circulation of air. The Palaeolithic fauna of the Ardèche will also become better known thanks to the abundance of animal bones and prints, and also from the drawings. Moreover, in the gigantic subsidence crater in the third chamber, the stratigraphic study of the floor will enable scientists to analyse the series of layers of sedimentary deposits, study the pollen and remains of charcoal they contain, and establish the successive occupations of this space. Thanks to the analysis of charcoal in the hearths, it will be possible to identify the types of wood used by Palaeolithic people. The study of the flints will also bring information about their stone tool industries. As for our knowledge of wall art, it is going to be revolutionized by the study of these depictions, a certain number of which had previously been very rare or totally unknown.

In none of the twenty-seven caves discovered in the gorges of the Ardèche has a single depiction of a rhinoceros ever been found, yet they are ubiquitous in Chauvet Cave. This leads us to suppose that the people of the Solutrean did not know or wish to depict this species. For our part, we are utterly convinced that the creation of the cave's works of art could date back to an even earlier period – as the radiocarbon dates now obtained indeed suggest (p. 122).

PROTECTION AND AUTHENTICATION

We were immediately aware of the exceptional scale of our discovery and its scientific significance. This imposed a great responsibility on us and a duty to protect the cave. During the first visits, as was our custom, we moved around with the greatest care on this precious floor, and only left a single trail, determined to avoid treading on certain soft areas; we probably walked more often in stockinged feet than in shoes. But we also had to prepare the cave for the visits of the state representatives and the scientists.

This is what we began to do on 24 December (fortunately, Jean-Marie and Christian were on vacation from 23 December until 3 January).

On 26 December, all three of us returned to the cave to continue our project of protection. We brought more plastic to carry on covering and demarcating all the trails (in all, more than 200 metres (650 ft) were unrolled), and placed lengths of fluorescent ribbon on the floor to mark the delicate areas next to the track, with teeth, skulls, bones and hearths. In the first chamber, where blocks have collapsed onto the floor – at the entrance to the Hall of the Bears – we stretched cords to mark the passage between the rocks, to avoid their being completely trampled. This methodical work occupied us for many long hours. That day, we also began climbing inside the cave, in search of an upper network in the first chamber: we wanted to be sure there was no other entrance.

And finally, on 28 December, once the cave was well protected, we announced our discovery to the Regional Administration of Cultural Affairs for the Rhône-Alps area. Jean-Marie telephoned Jean-Pierre Daugas, regional curator of Archaeology, because Mr Beghain, the director of the DRAC, was on holiday. The curator immediately realized the importance of the discovery because, even though this was a holiday period, Jean Clottes, an eminent specialist in Palaeolithic art, came to the Ardèche that same day to assess the cave.

So on 29 December, at Vallon-Pont-d'Arc, we met Jean Clottes, Jean-Pierre Daugas and Bernard Gély. Gély is in charge of archaeology at DRAC for the Drôme, the Ardèche and the Isère; we had known him for a long time because he had often visited caves we had discovered. Before entering the cavity, Jean Clottes, being sceptical,

52. A tiny, succinct sketch of a red rhinoceros, facing right. This rather crude animal was painted below and to the right of one of the facing rhinos in a marginal position. It provides evidence for the association of red and black paintings on certain panels.

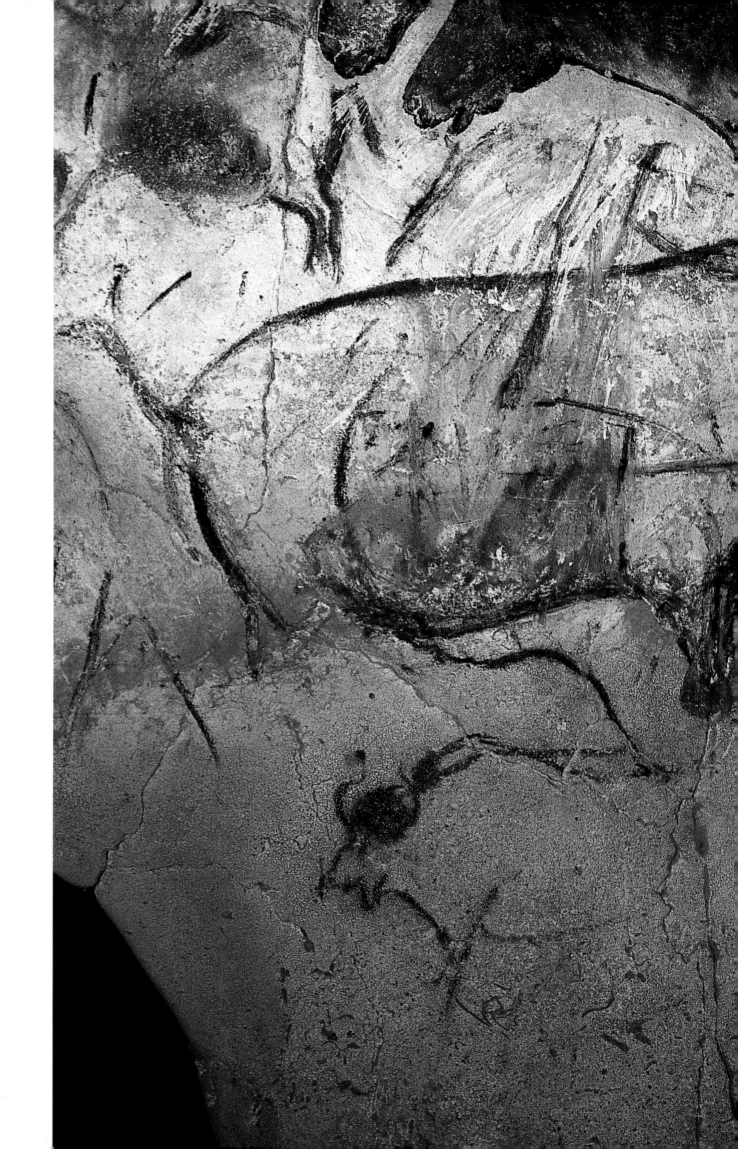

53. *The facing rhinoceroses.*
This scene is unique in
Palaeolithic art.

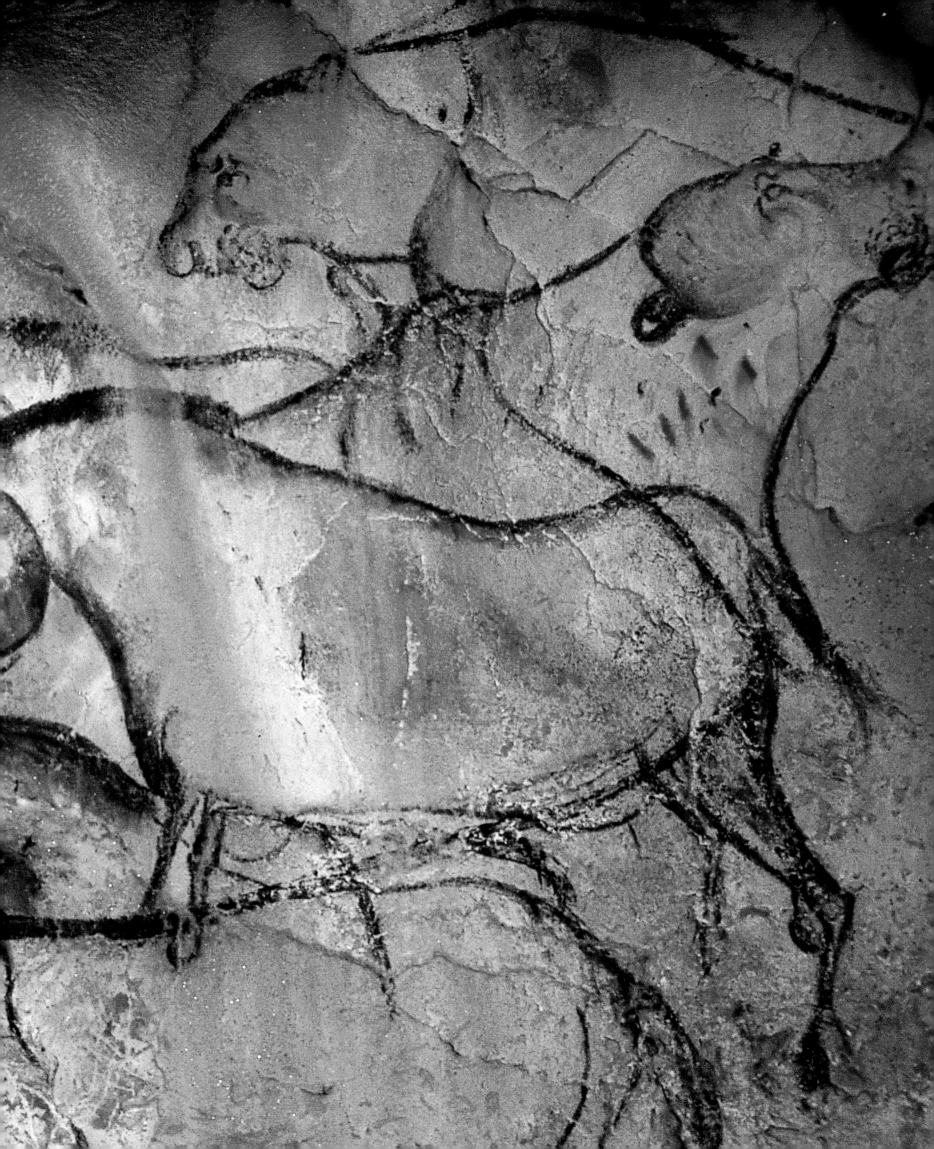

warned us that he had come to verify the authenticity of the paintings, adding mischievously that he was expecting to see some fakes. But Eliette promised him that, on leaving, we could all drink the champagne she had brought. And in fact the very first panel reassured him completely about the authenticity of the depictions. The film of calcite that covers certain panels and the subsidence beneath the owl left him in no doubt. We saw that he was profoundly moved by the extraordinary beauty of the paintings and engravings.

We spent the evening of New Year's Eve with the three friends who had been with us on 24 December, emotionally viewing the numerous slides of the cave and the video film we had made in it. We returned again on 2 January, with Michel Chabaud and Daniel André, to carry out an initial topographic survey by going along the trail and measuring the distance to the walls. On 13 January, we were summoned to the prefecture, and it was decided to install a door as soon as possible in order to give effective protection to the cave's entrance, by agreement with the owners who had been informed of the discovery. The cave's entrance, located in the commune of Vallon-Pont-d'Arc, is on private land.

From 13 January onward, the gendarmerie watched the cave day and night with great devotion, camping out in the glacial cold until the electronic alarm and the video surveillance system were installed. For our part we felt great relief, because until then our worries about seeing the cave damaged by inexperienced or unscrupulous visitors had been giving us sleepless nights. On 14 January, with the help of Mr Brunel, Eliette's father, we made a metal door, and a day later, having carried sand, water and cement up the cliff, we installed it at the entrance to the gallery, taking care to restore the same ventilation that there had been originally through the stones, so as to avoid modifying the cave's climatological equilibrium. A second door was added later, with the collaboration of our friend Michel Rosa (who subsequently joined us to complete the system of protection).

We were now ready for our discovery to be revealed. On 18 January we were in Paris, where a press conference had been organized at the Ministry of Culture. The minister Jacques Toubon made the official announcement of our discovery. Then we gave him a video cassette presenting the cave's masterpieces which we had filmed; its screening aroused the enthusiasm of the whole audience. Finally, we were subjected to the journalists' numerous questions.

Our main concern had always been to preserve the cave and deliver it intact, just as we discovered it, to humankind. Mission accomplished.

Previous double page:
54. Horses and lions on the left
wall of the central niche.

55. The heads of these horses facing each other were spared by the artist who painted the big feline. Conversely, the line of the feline's stomach crosses the breast of the horse at bottom right.

56. Detail of one of the horses on the right of the panel. Shading was used to give this head some relief.

57. The head of this horse, with its thick mane, was marked with red dots and lines, and was spared by the line of the stomach of the big lion on the right.

58. Detail of a horse head partially covered by a flow of calcite.

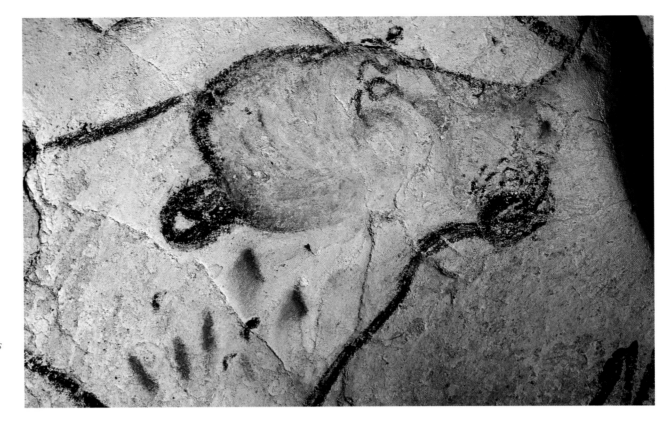

59. The head of the big feline, marked with red signs. The eye sockets are depicted with small undulating lines that recall those of the rhinoceroses' ears.

60. Detail of a bear or feline, its head seen three-quarter face and cut by the rump of an aurochs.

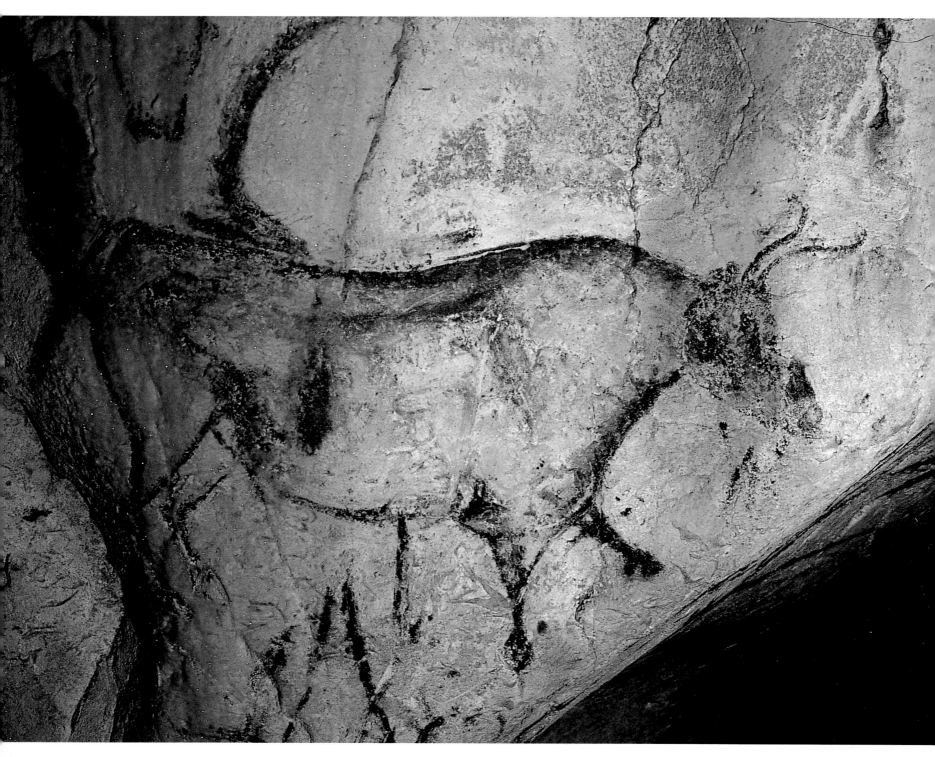

*62. An aurochs with its forelegs
spread apart, which recalls
certain cows at Lascaux, was
drawn on the right-hand wall
of the central niche in the
prolongation of the seven-
legged bison.*

63. Vertical animal with its head above the rump of the aurochs with spread forelegs. This could be a bear or a feline, but, curiously, the hoofs evoke those of a bison.

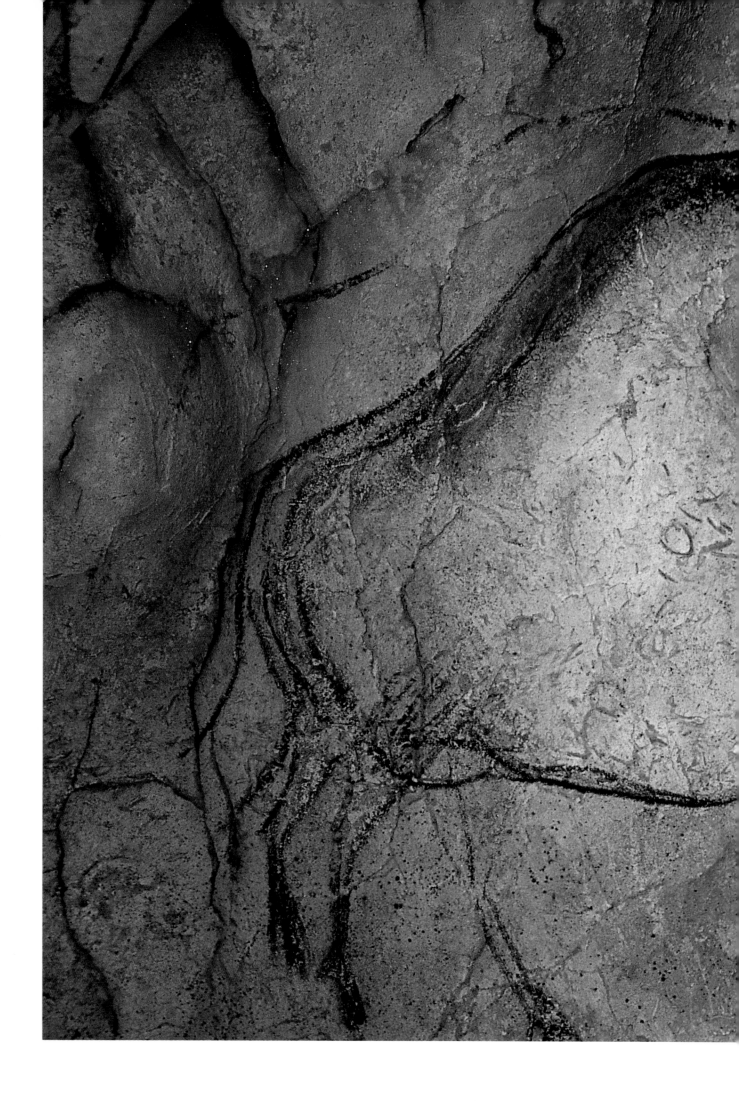

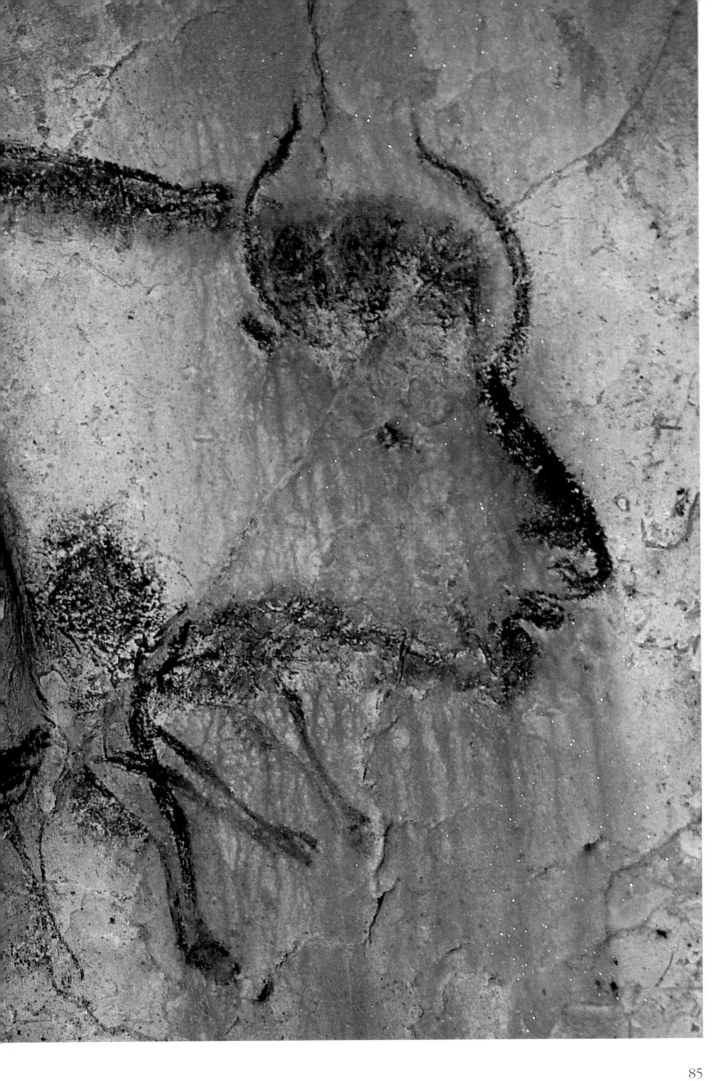

64. On the right wall of the central niche, opposite the big feline, a bison with multiple outlines was endowed with seven or eight legs, either to give it an effect of perspective or to indicate movement.

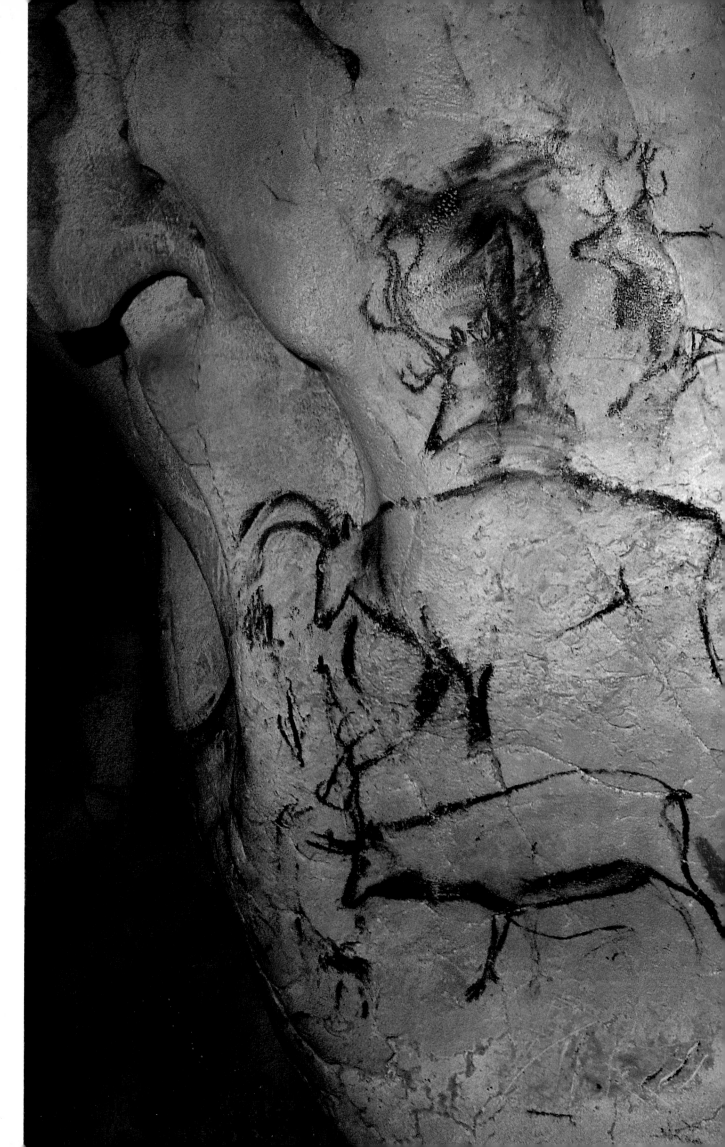

THE REINDEER
PANEL

65. *The whole of the Reindeer Panel. Besides an aurochs with forward-projecting horns, one can see a fairly crude horse head and a stiff bison with its belly moulded and Y-shaped legs, which recall the animals of Cosquer Cave.*

EPILOGUE: CHAUVET CAVE TODAY

Jean Clottes

Chauvet Cave was discovered only a matter of months ago. Its real study has not yet begun. But articles in the popular press giving the discoverers' first-impressions and publishing the first pictures have already caused an international sensation. No new cave since Lascaux has aroused such interest or so much admiration. Should we have waited for research to make significant progress and for the cave to be better known before presenting our findings in a book? These studies will take years in view of the complexity of the cave and the problems it poses. So a preliminary presentation has seemed preferable, even if it must necessarily remain incomplete and prove incorrect in some respects. There are many different stages in scientific understanding.

Where Chauvet Cave is concerned, we are still at the very beginning, so the analyses that follow are provisional. Interested readers will now have the first available assessment and numerous quality documents to help them share in, and better understand, the emotions of the discoverers and researchers when faced with one of the greatest masterpieces of Palaeolithic wall art.

AUTHENTICATION

Each discovery of prehistoric art, whatever its intrinsic importance, poses problems of authenticity.

Were the reported paintings or engravings made by Palaeolithic artists or could they be a hoax? Fakes in this field are rare, but they exist and can be clever. It required a long study by the Basque specialists Ignacio Barandiarán, Juan María Apellániz and Jesús Altuna to demonstrate that the numerous figures in the cave of Zubialde, near Vitoria, were fakes, since they were so carefully done: natural pigments had been used (iron oxides for the reds, manganese dioxide for the blacks), the animals and signs were known in other caves, and there was remarkable utilization of the natural contours for several animals.[1] On the other hand, when doubts were unfairly cast on Cosquer Cave, at Marseilles, the public believed for months that it was a hoax until research and analyses established its authenticity.[2] For all sorts of reasons, primarily a conservative tendency among us all when faced with the new, every great discovery has aroused its share of controversy and doubt. It happened with Altamira at the end of the last century, Lascaux in the 1940s, Rouffignac in the mid-1950s, and Cosquer in 1991 and 1992. Only Chauvet Cave seems to have escaped these suspicions.

One has to approach a new cave with caution. Everything has to be carefully verified, with one's critical faculties on the alert, before coming to a decision. After the discoverers had reported their find, what is called a visit of 'authentication' was

66. A reindeer with stiff legs. The line of the back of the upper reindeer is doubled, giving an effect of perspective that occurs often in Chauvet Cave.

organized very quickly, at the request of the Ministry of Culture and French-speaking Areas. As has been described in an earlier section, the visit took place on 29 December 1994, under the leadership of the discoverers, with Jean Clottes, specialist in Palaeolithic art, Jean-Pierre Daugas, regional curator of archaeology, and his associate Bernard Gély who has been working for years in the Ardèche caves. Later, on 7 February 1995, half a dozen French specialists and a Spanish special-ist (Javier Fortea) visited the cave and were able to see its paintings and engravings. None of them expressed the slightest doubt about them.

It is true that their physical aspect guaranteed the paintings' authenticity. When a painted line at Chauvet is examined with a magnifying glass, one sees that the apparently continuous and intact line in fact has innumerable tiny gaps due to ero-sion. A recent line will be much more coherent and continuous. As for the engraved lines, these will be clear, white and clean when the engravings are fresh, but full of micro-crystallizations after millennia on a cave's walls. In addition to observations of this kind, Chauvet Cave also had films of mineral deposits (concretions) or flows of calcite which covered paintings (plate 58); these were irrefutable testimony to the long time that has elapsed since the figures were drawn.

These observations alone would have been enough to establish the antiquity of the artworks, but there were others. For example, in one vast chamber, some overhanging rocks were covered with engravings, among which were an owl (plate 33) and a superb horse (plate 32). Originally these engravings were made by a standing adult, but today they are 5 metres (16 ft) above the ground because a gigantic subsidence has created a crater, 6 metres (20 ft) in diameter and 3 or 4 metres (10 or 13 ft) deep. If these engravings had been recent, they could only have been made by means of a big ladder which would have left traces, even assuming it could have been brought into the cave, which is impossible through the only known entrance.

The animal depictions themselves were above suspicion because of their quality and their naturalism. For them to have been faked would have required the combination of a great animal artist with an excellent knowledge of both Palaeolithic art and the animals of the period.

Finally, the very appearance of the floors destroyed any idea of deception. They were strewn with cave-bear bones. There were dozens of recognizable skulls (plate 38). Nothing had been touched. One could even make out the prints left by the bears during their movements around the cave, and the traces of their claws (plate 35). Thanks to the discoverers' precautions, everything was intact, and it was easy to see that the cave was virgin and devoid of shoe-prints, which would certainly have marked the soft floors if fakers had been at work in there, especially at the foot of certain decorated panels. So the art of Chauvet Cave was authentic, beyond any shadow of a doubt.

THE FLOORS

Not so very long ago, the price of every discovery was a series of destructions. In 1970, the first explorers of the Réseau Clastres at Niaux (Ariège) trampled – without seeing them – sixteen of the seventeen sandbanks with human footprints.[3] It was very rare that discoverers acted like Luc Wahl who, when he found Fontanet at Ornolac-Ussat-les-Bains, also in Ariège, immediately reported his discovery, so that it could be properly protect-ed. For a long time, prehistorians themselves used to contribute to the damage by picking up any remains seen on the surface in an attempt to date them and hence indirectly attribute a chronology to the figures on the walls. Often, hasty excavations completed the destruction of what survived. This is what happened at Lascaux[4] and in many other decorated caves.

Today, we have recognized the importance of the archaeological context for understanding

67. An aurochs was placed between depictions of reindeer. The reindeer above were partially erased.

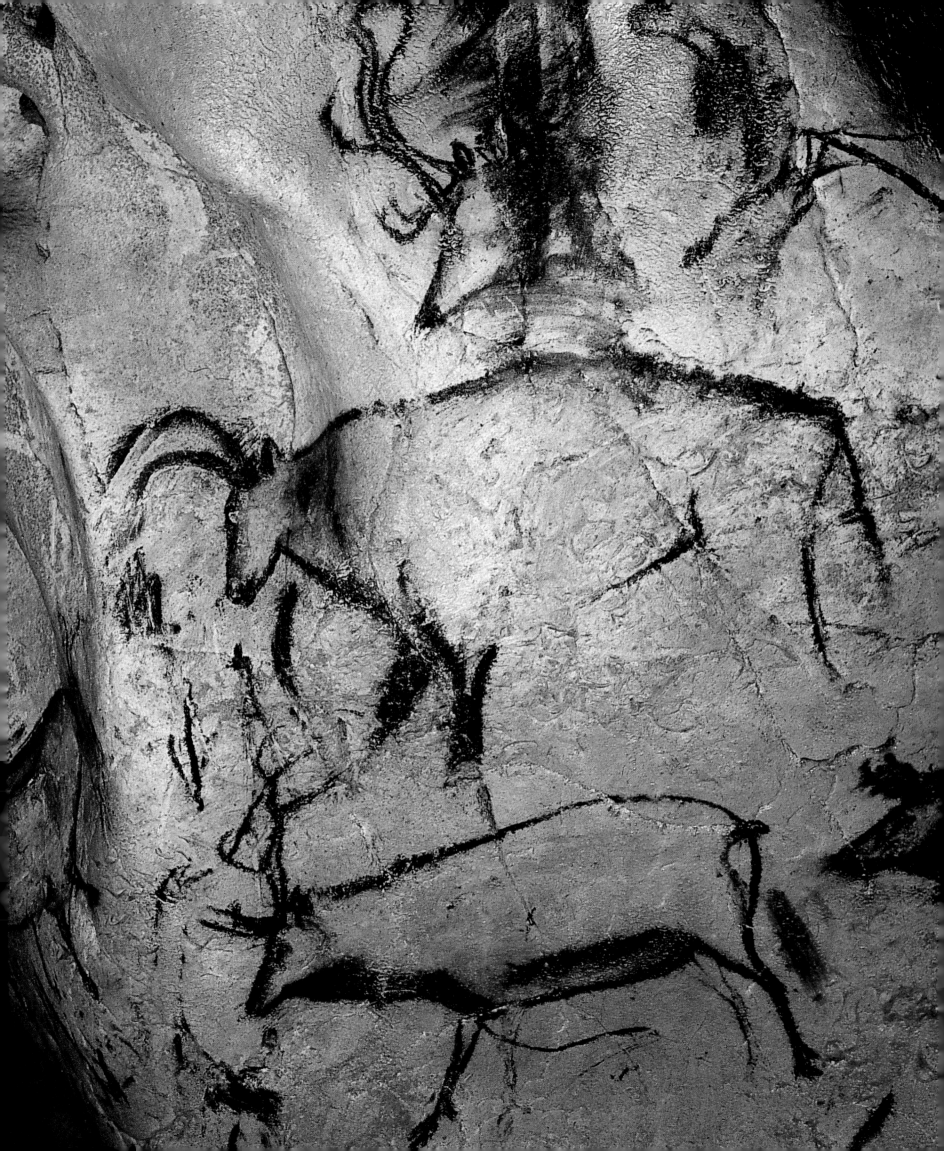

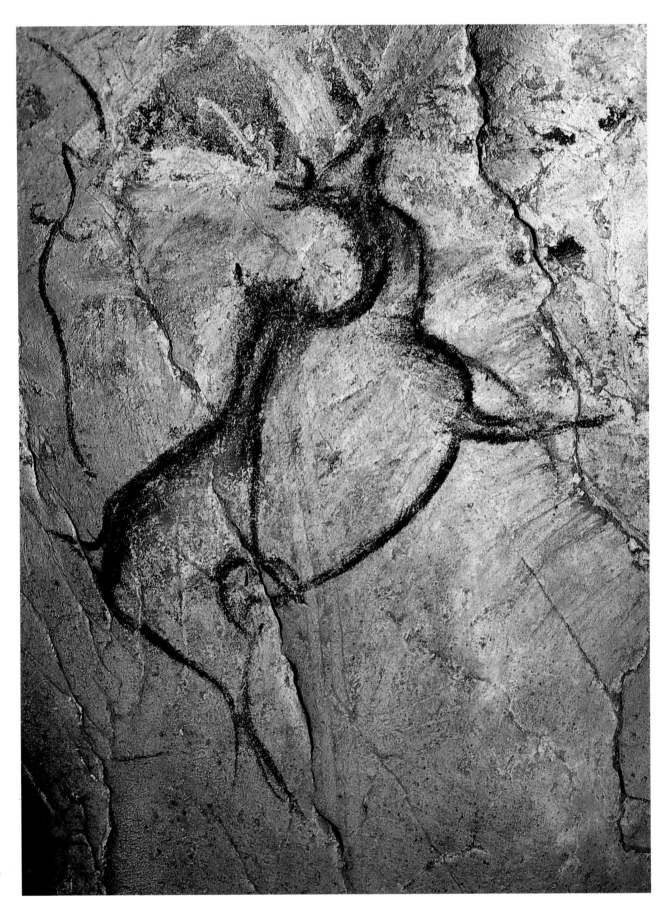

68. *A giant deer (megaceros)*
recognizable by its great hump.
To its left, the sketch of the back
of a rhinoceros has ears drawn
as double arcs, as is typical at
Chauvet. The wall was scraped
before the paintings were made.

69. *A rhinoceros with an*
enormous horn drawn in a
niche. Its horn follows the curve
of the wall.

70. Some horses, tiny
rhinoceroses below, and, to the
right, the front of a giant deer
(megaceros).

94

human activities in these caves.[5] The footprints enable us to know if children accompanied the adults and if the cave was frequented rarely or many times. Sometimes, objects were carefully placed, bones stuck into fissures, fires lit. These traces and these vestiges are all clues for research and study. In Chauvet Cave, most fortunately, everything remains to be done, everything is possible, thanks to the awareness and the intelligence of the explorers who picked up nothing and took pains not to damage the floors.

The first observation that comes to one's attention is that the cave's galleries were apparently not inhabited. A Palaeolithic habitation can easily be spotted, since the Aurignacians or Solutreans did not have our concern for hygiene; they left their garbage lying around, so that the floors

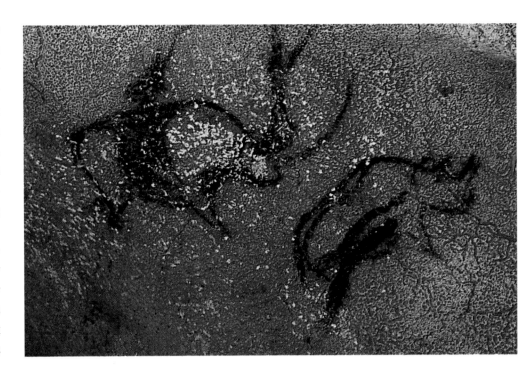

71. Under the stomach of the central horse two tiny rhinoceroses were drawn.

72. Two horses frame a giant deer (megaceros) with a big hump and stiff legs. Its antlers are not represented.

73. *A horse with a short head and thick, double mane like those of the horses at Lascaux.*

74. *An ibex with legs outstretched. The very developed horns are those of a relatively old male.*

large pieces of charcoal that are very well preserved. *A priori*, these heaps seem far more likely to have been removed from fireplaces than to be charcoal fallen from torches or abandoned on the spot where the fires burned.

Torches were unquestionably used by the prehistoric visitors, or at least by some of them. In several parts of the cave, the walls bear characteristic traces of the wiping of torches, which happens when the torch is turning to charcoal and is revived by being rubbed downwards against the rock. The contemporaneity of these torch marks and of the paintings remains to be determined. In at least one case, on the Panel of the Horses, the torch marks are later than the figures, since they are superimposed on the calcite that covers one animal's legs.

Another human action, and one that gave rise to vivid speculation in the media when the discovery was announced, is the placing of a bear skull on an isolated rock, in the chamber next to the Panel of the Horses, which we call the Skull Chamber (plates 34 and 44). People have talked of a 'bear cult', of the stone being engraved, carved and set in place. In fact, the block fell quite naturally from the ceiling and broke when it hit the ground. A bear skull was intentionally placed on it, but the stone has no trace of human workmanship. Two other bear skulls lie at the foot of the block and numerous others can be seen on the floor in this part of the cave. The absence of other bones could lead one to suppose that these skulls too were brought here for some unknown purpose. As for evoking a 'bear cult', it is a somewhat hasty interpretation, and involves jumping to highly premature conclusions. Cave bears are ubiquitous in Chauvet Cave. Their bones are everywhere, often scattered, sometimes heaped up – this may have been done by people, or the bones may have been carried by the bears themselves as they moved around, or by an influx of water. These points will have to be clarified by future research. Some skeletons are relatively well preserved, with vertebral

around their fireplaces were generally strewn with cut-up bones. There is nothing of the kind in Chauvet Cave, the usual refuse is nowhere to be seen. Of course one can speculate as to whether it may have been covered by deposits of clay, and whether excavations might unearth it. At first sight this seems most unlikely, because traces and vestiges of other kinds are visible; the floors do not therefore appear to have disappeared in the process of sedimentation following a hypothetical habitation.

Very few traces in the cave are attributable to Palaeolithic people. Some small depressions, about 50 centimetres (20 in) in diameter, contain charcoal in their blackened bases. It is possible that fires were made in them, but no trace of reddening can be seen. If there were fires, they were for lighting purposes, like those known elsewhere, for example in Cosquer Cave, and not hearths for cooking food. A dozen scattered flints have been observed. Future analyses will try to establish the provenance of the raw materials used to make these tools, and the nature of the wear patterns on the blades and flakes. Finally, numerous pieces of charcoal, identified by Stéphanie Thiébault (CNRS, Montpellier) as being Scots pine, have been observed in several heaps in the corridor joining the chamber of the Panel of the Horses with the End Chamber. These are

75. The black band in flat wash, depicted several times on the middle of rhinoceros bodies, represents the apparent division of the body into several sections delimited by folds of the thick hide.

76. An engraved rhinoceros. The lines were later enhanced with black.

columns still anatomically connected. In all, several dozen skulls have been observed. It is known that bears sometimes died during their hibernation, which would explain the profusion of skeletons in the caves that they regularly frequented. The bears left quantities of 'nests', great circular hollows, often marked by their claws or their fur. On the soft floors one can see veritable trails with remarkably clear footprints. The walls are festooned with clawmarks, some of which have had paintings and engravings made on top of them.

So it is certain that the bears came to this cave before the humans. This raises several questions. Did the human intrusions occur thousands of years after those of the bears, or did the prehistoric people come into the cave soon after the bears had left it? On one of the paintings, that of the three superimposed lions in the End Chamber (plate 79), it appears that clawmarks cut the animals' backs. This will have to be verified when it becomes possible to examine the drawings closely. If this were confirmed, it would mean that the bears returned to the cave after people had been here. This could explain the apparent absence of human prints on the soft floors, even though those of the bears are well preserved. One hypothesis could be that the artists' prints have been erased by influxes of water before the bears began using the cave again. The studies of the floors will doubtless attach particular importance to elucidating the relationship between the people and the bears, as well as establishing precisely which activities were carried out in the cave. For example, was a superb ibex skull (plate 36) found a few dozen metres from the entrance to the cave deliberately placed there? And why were two bear bones stuck into the floor of the cave? Many questions remain unanswered.

Double page overleaf:

77. The right wall of the End Chamber has several black animals, including two rhinoceroses, an incomplete horse head, a bear and multiple engravings that have not yet been deciphered.

THE THEMES

As in all the Palaeolithic decorated caves, the chosen themes comprise mostly geometric signs and animals.

The Signs

Although signs are relatively few in number when compared with those in the caves of the Pyrenees, Périgord or Cantabria, they are far more abundant in Chauvet Cave than in any other cave in the Ardèche group. The absence of signs directly placed on animal figures is a very typical Ardéchois feature, in contrast to caves like Niaux or Cosquer. For the moment, the only examples are a long unbarbed line on one of the engraved ibex behind the Panel of the Horses (plate 42), and, on this frieze, five short red stripes on the outstretched neck of a fine lion and a red dot on its snout (plate 59), as well as two red dots and a short red line on the muzzle of a horse (plate 55). Just behind the first reindeer near the Panel of the Horses, a wide vertical red line is partially doubled by a much fainter one (plate 67). A few black lines here and there, for example on one of the facing rhinoceroses (plate 53), may or may not be real signs. Undoubtedly, future study will perhaps decide this question and enable us to make out signs that are currently lost in the jumble of depictions. It would be surprising if no ambiguities remain. For instance, just under the snout of a rhinoceros, to the right of the Lion Panel in the End Chamber, half a dozen red lines (plate 88, top right) can be interpreted as a complex sign or as the animal's breath, or even as blood falling from its muzzle. In addition, the big bison just to the right of the niche in the Lion Panel (plate 81) is marked on its head and front by a dozen oblique parallel lines, as if someone had wanted to obliterate it.

On the left of this great Lion Panel, between the group of rhinoceroses and that of the felines, one can see a dozen big red dots in a semi-circle (plate 87), as well as a dozen little red dots in a line, plus two other red spots. These dots seem to be associated with some scarcely visible red animal figures that preceded the black paintings. This poses the problem – to which we shall return again later – of the chronological relationship between the red and black figures.

Some big red dots are isolated. Others mark the edge of certain red panels, like that of the panther. The big black panel at the end contains a red mark, beneath the head of the rhinoceros at the bottom. However, the red signs are far more numerous and varied in the entrance chambers. The most frequent and characteristic signs are the groups of circular dots, 6–8 centimetres (2–3 in) in diameter. They form all kinds of configurations, from little groups of dots arranged vertically or in a rectangle in fives or sixes, to sheets of them that can vary from ten (plate 11) to a hundred dots or more, with three major concentrations. One of these evokes an animal shape, perhaps a bison or a mammoth (plate 8). Another occupies almost the whole of a hanging rock (plate 13). The third, on the left-hand wall, 20 metres (65 ft) from the entrance, extends for several metres and ends on the right with two crosses which frame a barely visible sign with numerous lateral appendages (plates 7 and 9). These panels of big red dots are strongly reminiscent of those at Pech-Merle, in the Lot.

The other red signs in these chambers are sometimes found in other Ardèche caves, like stripes, short or long, in twos or threes, or a semi-circle of little dots – as on the Panel of the Positive Hands (plate 26) – or even boomerang-like shapes. Some are quite original: the most extraordinary are in the same area, and it is hard to say whether they are really signs or stylized animals. Two of them occupy the bottom of a hanging rock; they look like butterflies or headless birds with wings that are too wide (plate 24); two identical signs are visible on the wall opposite, near a bizarre depiction with a massive, elongated rectangular body extended by two

78. Animal engravings, including that of a big feline, on the right wall of the End Chamber.

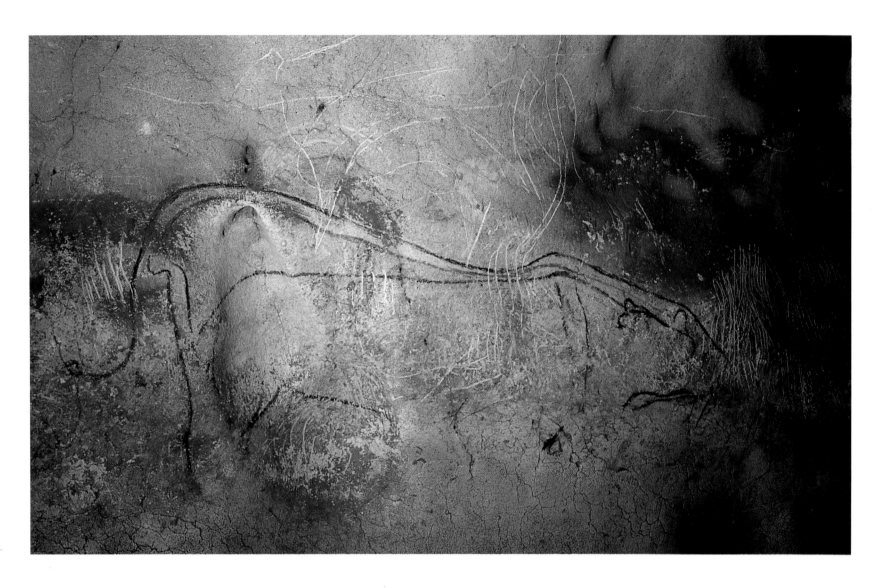

vertical antennae and the whole thing is crossed horizontally by six more or less undulating lines (plate 16); is this a sign or an insect?

The Animals

The animal depictions on which the following observations are based are numerous: 216 figures, including those of all techniques. But the cave has not yet been completely studied, and indeed is far from having been entirely explored, because of the soft floors which need to be preserved. This prevents a complete examination of the recesses, and the remote walls and ceilings. The total number of animals will probably be around 300, perhaps more. The discoverers have already counted 267 animals, and they will find others. However, the 216 identified during an initial count provide a usable statistical base that enables one to make some preliminary remarks.

The rhinoceros is strongly predominant: there are 47, about a quarter (22%) of all the animal figures. The black ones (38) are far more frequent than the red (7) or the engraved ones (2, including one accentuated with black). They have several points in common that make them look like a homogeneous group: characteristic ears in double arcs, like little wings (plate 80), on both sides of the cervico-dorsal line, ball-like feet, a broad black median stripe dividing the body in the middle; several of them (two red, some black, including those in perspective on the Lion Panel) have a front horn that is disproportionately long.

The lions are the next most abundant: 36 (17%), including 28 black, 7 red and 1 engraved. On the Lion Panel (plates 81 and 87), where they are particularly numerous, only their fronts and outstretched heads are represented. The fangs are never depicted, but on the complete animals the little tuft of hair at the end of the tail is regularly drawn. None of them has the mane that one commonly associates with male lions, because of those in Africa; no doubt, like the other felines, the cave lions did not have one. None of the lions depicted in Palaeolithic art have a mane, despite the patently male character of a few figures: for example, in Chauvet Cave, the very big lions drawn in perspective in the End Chamber have their scrotum depicted (plate 79).

The mammoths (34), so frequent in the caves of the Ardèche group, represent 16% of the animals, all techniques included: 4 red, 9 black, 21 engraved. Whatever the technique used, they are mostly characterized by the depiction of the belly and the inner side of the legs with a single horseshoe-shaped line. It appears that the mammoth on the right-hand edge of the niche in the centre of the Lion Panel (plate 83) is young and ungainly, with enormous ball-shaped feet.

There are 26 horses (12%). Red ones are rare (2), and black ones (18) dominate, as for most of the animals; some are engraved (4), and two tiny little heads were even painted in yellow (plate 10), the only paintings of that colour in the cave. Whatever the technique used, the horses have broad manes that form a thick mass. One engraved horse bears two stripes on its shoulder (plate 32), and another, also engraved, has a flattened M-shaped line that marks the difference in colour between the belly and the flank (plate 29), a convention that appears in Cosquer Cave and Lascaux before becoming all the rage during the Magdalenian.

The 19 bison (9%) are all black; one of them was engraved before being enhanced with black. Drawn on the Panel of the Horses, the Lion Panel and in the corridor inbetween, they look very alike. They have a very thick and bushy mane, a head seen in three-quarter view or full-face with eyes and horns seen from the front. On a rocky ridge of the great Lion Panel, 4 isolated heads, drawn full-face, have been superimposed (plates 82 and 83).

The bears (12, i.e. 5.5%), in contrast with the other animals, are more often red (8) than black (3); 1 is engraved. These are cave bears, recognizable from the 'stop' (a marked break of slope that separates the brow from the muzzle), rather than brown bears.

The 10 reindeer (5%) are all black. With one exception (the reindeer on the Lion Panel), they are all grouped in two places: near the Panel of the Horses where, rather curiously, several have been partially erased (plate 67), and on a hanging rock in the next chamber (plate 39), the one with the skull placed on a stone.

Other animals are few in number: 7 black aurochs, all on the Panel of the Horses (plate 50) or in its immediate vicinity; 7 ibex (including five engraved in different stages of abbreviation immediately behind the Panel of the Horses, plus

80. A little rhinoceros with the interior of its outline shaded, in the centre of the Panel of the Horses. Note the double arc of the ears, identical to those of the numerous rhinoceroses in Chauvet Cave.

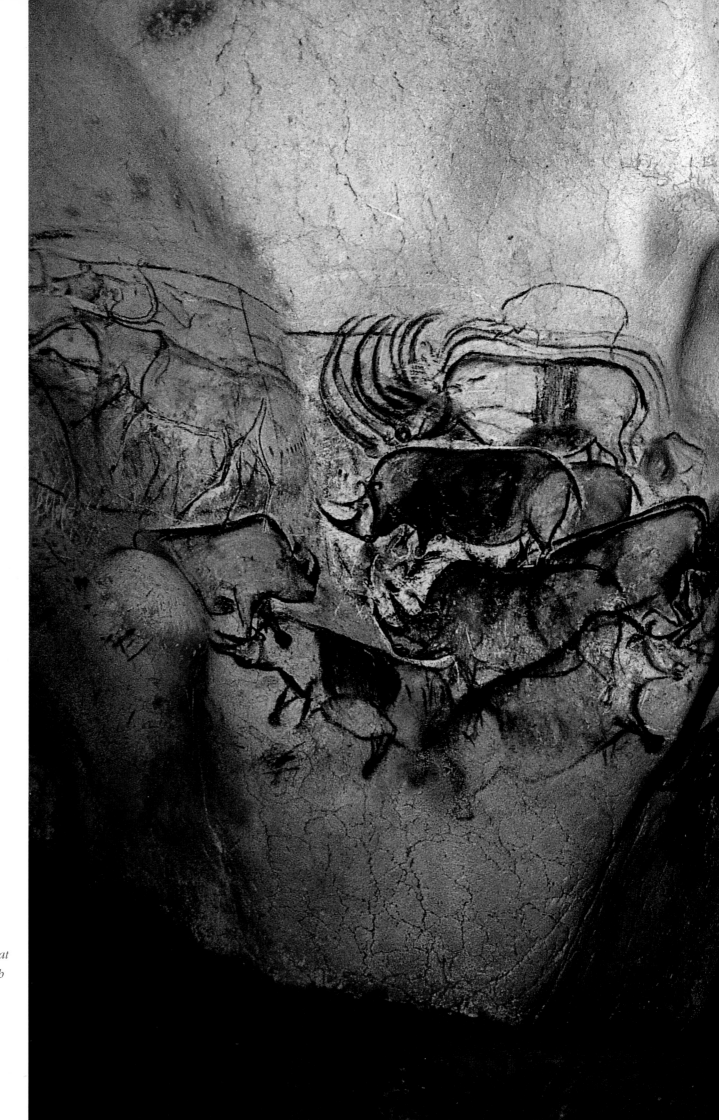

THE LION PANEL

81. *This big panel presents a composition comparable to that of the Panel of the Horses, with an accumulation of different animals on either side of a central niche.*

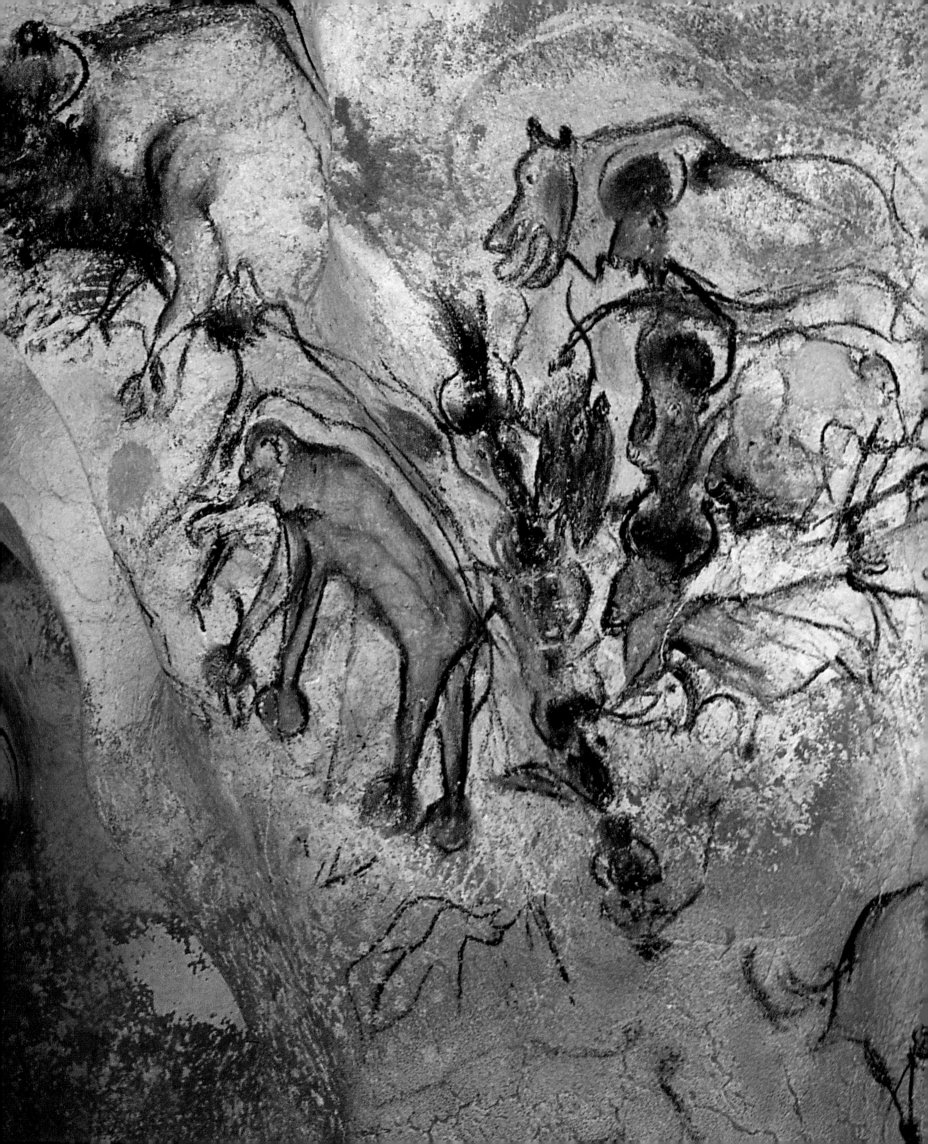

one red and one black); 3 black megaceros stags in one corridor, recognizable from their prominent withers, even though they do not have the enormous antlers of the males (plates 68 and 72); a red stag; a red ́panther (plate 23), the first depiction of this animal in Palaeolithic art, as is an engraving of an owl identifiable as a great horned owl (plate 33); a red animal, above the panther, has the same head as the bears, but it stands taller on its paws and the front of the body is spotted, which has led to its being called a hyena (plate 23); and finally, 11 animals (2 red, 7 black, 2 engraved, i.e. 5%) remain indeterminate for the moment.

Among the most numerous animals – those which are rare elsewhere – the rhinoceroses, lions, and mammoths seem to be distributed indiscriminately throughout the cave, and they are depicted using different techniques. The horses are mostly black, and the bears primarily red, but with notable exceptions. Conversely, bison, aurochs, reindeer and megaceros stags are exclusively black and are found only in the deep chambers and galleries.

On the great panels, deliberate groupings can be observed: animals of the same species are facing each other (the 2 rhinoceroses); in a row (4 red rhinoceroses; cf. plate 27); partially superimposed and facing in the same direction (the 4 fine horses of plate 51, the aurochs on the same panel, two groups of 3 lions in the End Chamber); or indeed in dense groups, with an identical outstretched posture (the lions on the right of the Lion Panel, facing towards a group of bison; the lions on the left of the same panel), or giving an impression of a crowd (the rhinoceroses on the other side of the Lion Panel; cf. plate 86). One begins to wonder if these are not actual scenes. The animals are often depicted in action, which is not so common in Palaeolithic wall art. One bison has 7 or 8 legs, no doubt to evoke movement (plate 64); not far from it, an aurochs has its front legs spread apart and recalls certain cows in Lascaux (plate 62); some lions

appear to be stalking (plate 84), and some reindeer are running, their heads held high (plate 65).

Human Representations

Everyone knows that humans are extremely rare in Palaeolithic art. Chauvet Cave is no exception, since not one image of a complete human figure has been found there yet. There are only some segments of the body and one composite being.

In the entrance chambers, a panel of red paintings contains three negative hands, made by spitting paint in the stencil technique, and five positive hand prints (plates 25 and 26). The latter are much rarer in wall art: for example, there is one in Cosquer Cave. On another panel, not far from the previous one, four negative hands are associated with red dots and a sketchy black horse (plate 28). None of these negative hands (plate 91) has incomplete fingers. In the gallery that leads from the Panel of the Horses to the End Chamber, the Megaceros Gallery, two big pubic triangles, with the vulva indicated, have been engraved.

Finally, a few metres from the Lion Panel at the end, and opposite it, a hanging rock has two black felines and a horse on one side, and, on the other side, a black creature, upright and leaning slightly forward: the top of its body is that of a bison, and the bottom that of a human, with the two legs well indicated. This being occupies all the available space, and faces the Lion Panel. It is this figure that one sees first when one arrives in the chamber (plate 93). In front of the body a sort of filled triangle has been painted, point downward, with a very concave base emphasized with a mark. This extraordinary individual inevitably evokes the 'sorcerers' of Les Trois-Frères in the Ariège and Gabillou in the Dordogne.

THE PICTORIAL TECHNIQUES

The different techniques were not brought into play at random. We have seen that most of the

Previous double page:
82. Right part of the great Lion Panel, with numerous lions heading towards some bison.

83. On the right-hand side of the central niche, a young mammoth is depicted with legs ending in spheres and a double upper outline. To its right, several bison heads were drawn full face on the rocky ridge.

110

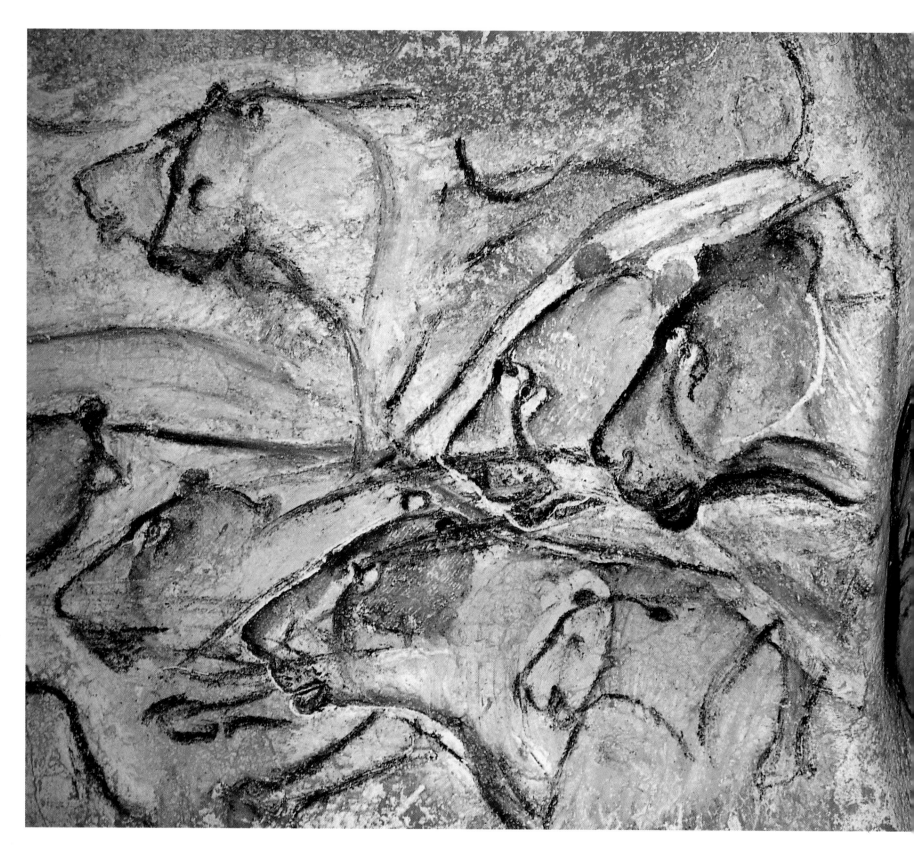

84. Detail of the lions on the
right of the Lion Panel.

red signs are in the chambers close to the entrance. The same is true of most of the red animals known at present (33 red and only 3 black, with no engravings). On the other hand, 21 engraved animals (including 3 enhanced with black) and 140 black animals are in the more distant chambers, with only one definite red animal. The artists therefore preferred to use the deep parts of the cave for the accumulation of either engraved or black images, while the colour red was preferred near the entrance. This, of course, poses the question of the chronological or religious value of the chosen techniques. We shall return to this problem later.

All viewers have noticed the naturalism of the figures and the reality of the postures. The

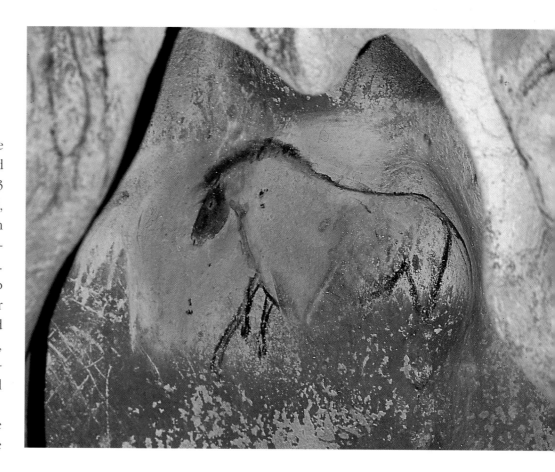

85. The horse at the back of the niche in the middle of the Lion Panel.

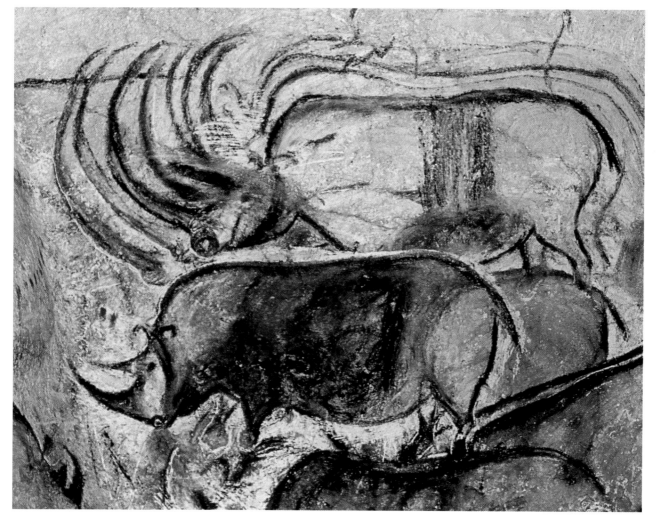

86. The herd of rhinoceroses seen in perspective.

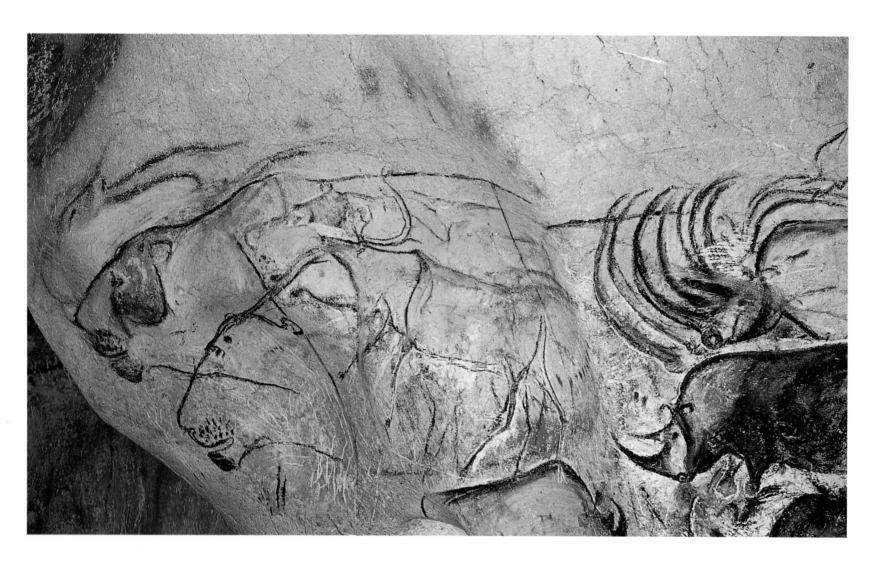

87. *The lions on the left of the Lion Panel. One can just make out some earlier red dots and lines.*

88. *On the left wall, to the right of the Lion Panel, two lion heads are surmounted by a rather extraordinary bison: it was drawn on a dihedron, the head is seen full-face, while the body, in profile, is at 90 degrees to the head, which accentuates the effect of perspective.*

animals are easily recognizable for the most part, since the indeterminate ones only account for 5% of the total. These are not stereotyped images which were transcribed to convey the concept 'lion' or 'rhinoceros', but living animals faithfully reproduced. This was done thanks to several techniques, perfectly mastered and systematically put into practice.

The most obvious of these is the rendering of perspective. In many cases, the heads or bodies of the animals more or less overlap, doubtless to give an effect of numbers, unless it is a depiction of movement. This quest for perspective can be found half a dozen times among the black paintings, and at least once for engravings (two superimposed mammoths), but never among the red paintings seen so far. Some refinements are

visible: for example, on the Panel of the Horses, the contours of the lion with an outstretched head stop six times on contact with the pre-existing three horses, so that the animal appears to be partially hidden by their bodies (plate 54).

Some of the walls were prepared by scraping before being drawn upon so that the images would stand out better. Examples include the Panel of the Horses, the megaceros at the entrance of the corridor leading to the End Chamber (plate 68) and, in the latter, some parts of the Lion Panel. Here, to highlight certain animals, some contours were outlined by scraping, which gives an effect of white and of relief (seen in the rhinoceros group; compare also the horn of the rhinoceros to the right (plate 90) on the Panel of the Horses).

89. On an overhang, three lions were sketched in perspective.

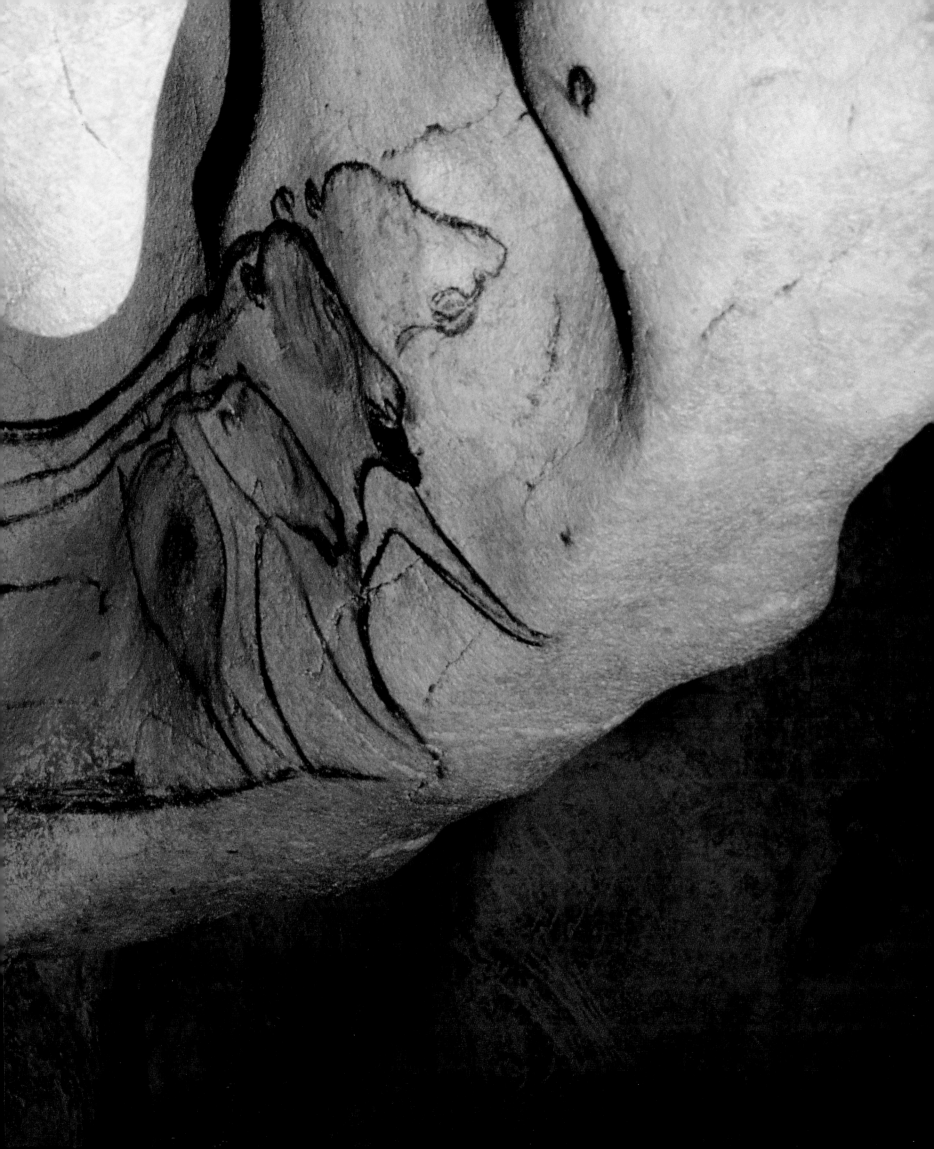

Another very frequent procedure in Chauvet Cave, extremely rare or unknown elsewhere, is that of shading. It consists of spreading the paint with the hand or a tool to obtain gradations that enable the artist to depict relief or the nuances of the animal's coat. The four superimposed horse heads are the most dazzling example, but this procedure was even used for some red paintings of rhinoceroses and bears in the Hall of the Bears.

HOW OLD ARE THE PAINTINGS?

After the question of authenticity, the major problem posed by the discovery of wall art is that of its date (or dates). Preliminary radiocarbon analyses have recently become available (see below), throwing up remarkable results. First analyses, however, let us attempt a stylistic analysis to see what chronological information this may yield.

There is virtually no doubt that all the images cannot have been produced by the same person in a single episode. Some clumsy and stiff drawings – for example, on the right of the Panel of the Horses, a horse head and a bison with Y-shaped legs (plate 65) – coexist with depictions that display mastery and sureness of touch: they were not made by the same artists. One can even discern successive phases: on the left of the Lion Panel, vague red traces can just be distinguished (plate 87). They have been largely erased, and are overlain by big lion heads. Finally, people came into the cave some time after the production of the black paintings, because torch wipes, which are not covered by concretions, are superimposed on the calcite that covers certain drawings. Analyses of the charcoal on the floors will give chronological indications, but will not provide any proof: these pieces of charcoal might have been left at the moment when some paintings were produced, but it is equally possible that they could be earlier or later by several millennia.

At first sight, the red paintings seem different from the black, and one might be tempted to

consider them as older, on the basis of the erased traces in the Lion Panel and of the less accomplished and often rougher nature of the red animals. However, an attentive examination reveals some striking convergences between red and black figures. To begin with, in the choice of themes: rhinoceroses, felines and bears are rare animals in Palaeolithic wall art. Yet here they are depicted as frequently with one technique as with the other. If there were millennia separating the red and black paintings, one would have to deduce that the more recent artists had copied – in the deep chambers – the original themes of their predecessors, only leaving a few black paintings near the entrance, whereas the first artists had done the opposite: they would have limited themselves to the entrance areas and drawn only a few very rare figures in the depths.

There are other arguments against the colours having chronological value. In one composition in the end part of the cave, comprising three identical big felines superimposed in the same taut posture (plate 79), the one in the middle is red whereas the other two are black. In this case, it is established that the red was used concurrently with the black by the same artist. In the same part of the cave, a black rhinoceros is overpainted with red lines under the snout and has red horns. Red dots and dashes, as we have seen, also mark a black horse and feline in the Panel of the Horses, and a little red rhinoceros was painted just behind the facing rhinoceroses (plate 52).

Finally, similar conventions or processes were used in both cases and reveal a close community of concepts. For example, one of the original features of the numerous black rhinoceroses is the way in which the ears were depicted, as a double arc (plate 80); and the red rhinoceroses in a line on the Panel of the Positive Hands have identical ears. Moreover, certain rhinoceroses, red and black, display a front horn of exaggerated length. Another example: shading, used so often and with so much precision in the black animals, was also used to great effect for some red bears and rhinoceroses.

90. Detail of the facing rhinoceroses. Note the little ears drawn as double arcs.

All these common points lead one to think that even if it was not the same people who used the reds and blacks, and even if these colours could have had a different value, their users did not belong to successive cultures that were widely separated in time. Comparisons with caves elsewhere shed some further light on the matter

At first glance, the clouds of big red dots evoke Pech-Merle, in the Lot. The comparison of the Solutrean caves of the Ardèche with those of the Lot, particularly Pech-Merle and Cougnac, was made long ago by Jean Combier.[6] In Chauvet Cave, other observations point the same way, such as the yellow used for the little horse heads, because this colour is 'manifestly more abundant' in Solutrean paintings than in Magdalenian ones from Quercy and in Cantabria.[7] Negative hands

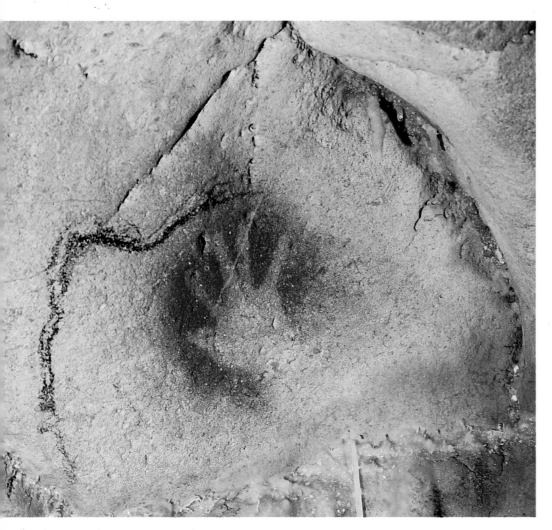

91. One of the hand stencils in Chauvet Cave. In contrast to Gargas or Cosquer Cave, the fingers are complete in all the hands depicted.

(plate 91) are also present at Pech-Merle, in association with red dots. Moreover, they might be older than the Solutrean, since at Pech-Merle a row of bent thumbs, seen in profile, depicted in negative and hence to be linked to the hands, is identical to the row of thumbs at Gargas; and at Gargas, the negative hands are attributed to the Perigordian, about 27,000 years ago. At Pech-Merle, as at Cougnac, the megaceros stag was depicted. The presence of this rare species also justifies a comparison with the second phase, dated to 18,500–19,200 years ago, at Cosquer Cave,[2] 150 kilometres (100 miles) from Chauvet. Like those of Cosquer, the bison of the Ardèche cave systematically display heads seen from the front or three-quarter face, with both eyes and horns in frontal perspective (plate 82). The animals' legs are sometimes identically simplified, in a 'Y' shape, a characteristic abbreviation (plate 65) also present at Ebbou.

Other elements certainly echo the Solutrean caves of the Ardèche. These include the S-shaped horns of the aurochs on the Panel of the Horses (plate 50), very similar to those of the engraved aurochs at Ebbou.[8] Even more characteristic are the tapering muzzle (like a duck's bill) of the engraved horse with a double stripe on its shoulder[9] (plate 32), and the arched or horseshoe-shaped belly of the mammoths (plate 30), very frequent in the Ardèche caves (Chabot, Les Deux-Ouvertures), where it is considered typical of the local Solutrean depictions,[10] whereas elsewhere it is far more ancient (Jovelle, in the Dordogne).

More distant comparisons also evoke a pre-Magdalenian period. For example, the two engraved vulvas of Chauvet Cave are identical to those of Micolón, in Asturias, a tiny cave with a Solutrean archaeological context, and which is attributed to this culture.[11] Conversely, certain details make one think of Lascaux, generally dated to 17,000 years ago and to an archaic Magdalenian, but which has certain paintings that could be more ancient. Apart from the aesthetic quality of the ensemble, it is the thick manes of

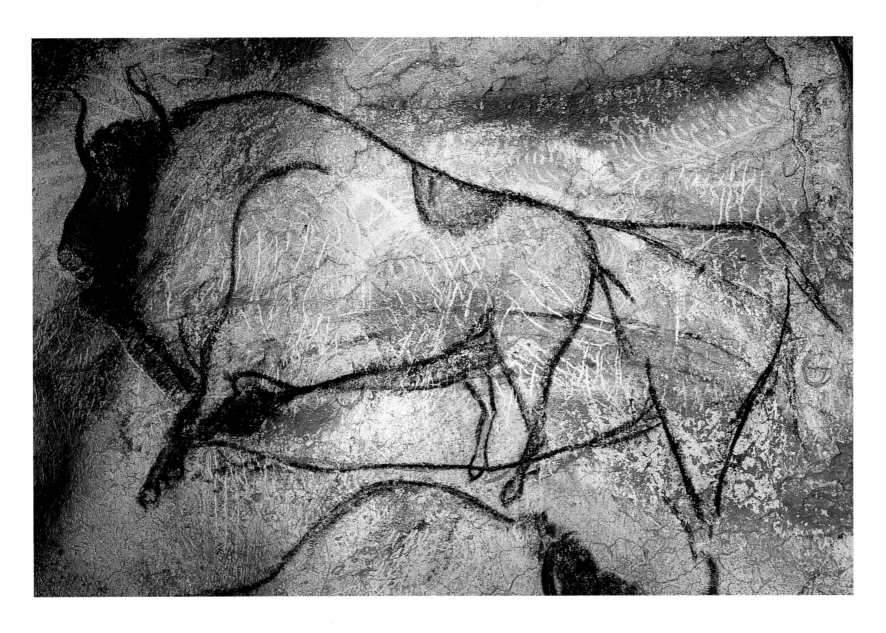

the horses, sometimes doubled (plate 73), the ball-shaped feet of certain animals, the depiction of perspective for legs, the internal modelling through the effects of flat colouring, the technique of leaving the nostril or eye white, and the animation of some subjects that recall Lascaux. A big bison in the central niche of the Panel of the Horses, which has seven or eight legs (plate 64), evokes the walking ibex depicted in the rock-shelter of Le Colombier II, at Vallon-Pont-d'Arc, where they are dated to the Middle Magdalenian. However, the fact that the bison's upper outline is tripled suggests an attempt to convey perspective rather than movement.

After this stylistic analysis, a tentative bracket between 17,000 and 21,000 years ago or earlier was considered plausible. However, before the radiocarbon dates became available I stated that the powerful originality of Chauvet Cave made dating surprises a distinct possibility.

THE RADIOCARBON DATES FROM CHAUVET CAVE

The above-mentioned surprises came sooner than expected. The stylistic comparisons remain of great interest, but some dates obtained by the

92. A big black bison superimposed on clawmarks and engravings, including those of two horses, on a wall perpendicular to the Lion Panel.

121

Centre des Faibles Radioactivités at Gif-sur-Yvette (CNRS-CEA, France) from tiny samples taken from three paintings done with charcoal (the two rhinoceroses (plate 90) and the big bison (plate 92)) proved to be far older than anticipated.

These paintings produced the following ages: 32,410 ± 720 BP (BP = before the present) and 30,790 ± 600 BP for the right-hand rhinoceros, 30,940 ± 610 BP for the left-hand one, and 30,340 ± 570 BP for the big bison. It should be stressed that radiocarbon dates are statistical estimates, with a standard deviation, which means that the 'true' date has a 68% chance of being within the timespan indicated by the ± sign. To have a 95% chance, one has to double this span (two standard deviations, SD). The difference between the measured ages of the right-hand rhinoceros is not significant at two SD. The dates of the three figures are statistically compatible, and show that they were produced in the same period, within a timespan of 1300 years, centred on 31,000 years ago.

The samples from two different torch marks, in separate chambers, were dated to 26,980 ± 410 BP and 26,980 ± 420 BP for one, and 26,120 ± 400 BP for the other. These results are equivalent and indicate that the torch wipes occurred about 4000 years after the production of the paintings. The first of the two was superimposed on the calcite covering an animal on the panel of the facing rhinoceroses; we already knew that it corresponded to a human visit much later than the production of these paintings, and the measurements have confirmed and quantified this observation.

As for the samples taken from the floor, they were analyzed by the Laboratoire du Radiocarbone de Lyon and the Research Laboratory for Archaeology and History of Art at Oxford. The charcoal from the Megaceros Gallery – in great quantity and in an excellent state of conservation – gave a date of 29,000 ± 400 BP, very close to that obtained for the paintings. The other two measurements from charcoal had to be obtained from smaller quantities. They are relatively less

precise, and the two dates (24,770 ± 780 BP and 22,800 ± 400 BP) may therefore indicate contemporaneity.

So a series of dating tests were carried out under perfectly controlled experimental conditions, by three different laboratories. In some cases, it was possible to test the reliability of the analyses by taking two independent measurements from the same sample.

These dates can be grouped in three distinct age clusters:

– around 31,000 BP for samples taken directly from the paintings; the date of 29,000 BP for the big pieces of charcoal from the End Chamber is not significantly different.

– around 26,500 BP for samples from the torch marks.

– around 24,000 BP for two other charcoal samples from the floor.

The dates show that the cave had several human incursions, separated by a few millennia. The first, about 31,000 years ago, was when some paintings were done, which are therefore much older than anticipated. More recent incursions occurred between 27,000 and 23,000 years ago, but we do not yet know if these latter visits involved the production of wall art or not. Future research will have to establish this. Certainly, the results obtained so far do not mean that Chauvet Cave is dated. Only three drawings have been analyzed, out of more than three hundred. It is by no means impossible that other paintings or engravings were made later.

However, the constant repetition of the same conventions in representing animals of the same species probably indicates that they were not drawn in very different periods. As we have seen, the rhinoceroses – including the two that have been dated – always had ears in the form of two little arcs joined together, and all the bison display horns seen from the front surmounted by a thick mane. These and many other observations argue for a certain unity. This means that many figures must have been produced in the same

93. A hanging rock, perpendicular to the Lion Panel, is entirely filled on the side visible from the entrance by the representation of a composite being, half human for the bottom part of the body, and half bison for the upper part.

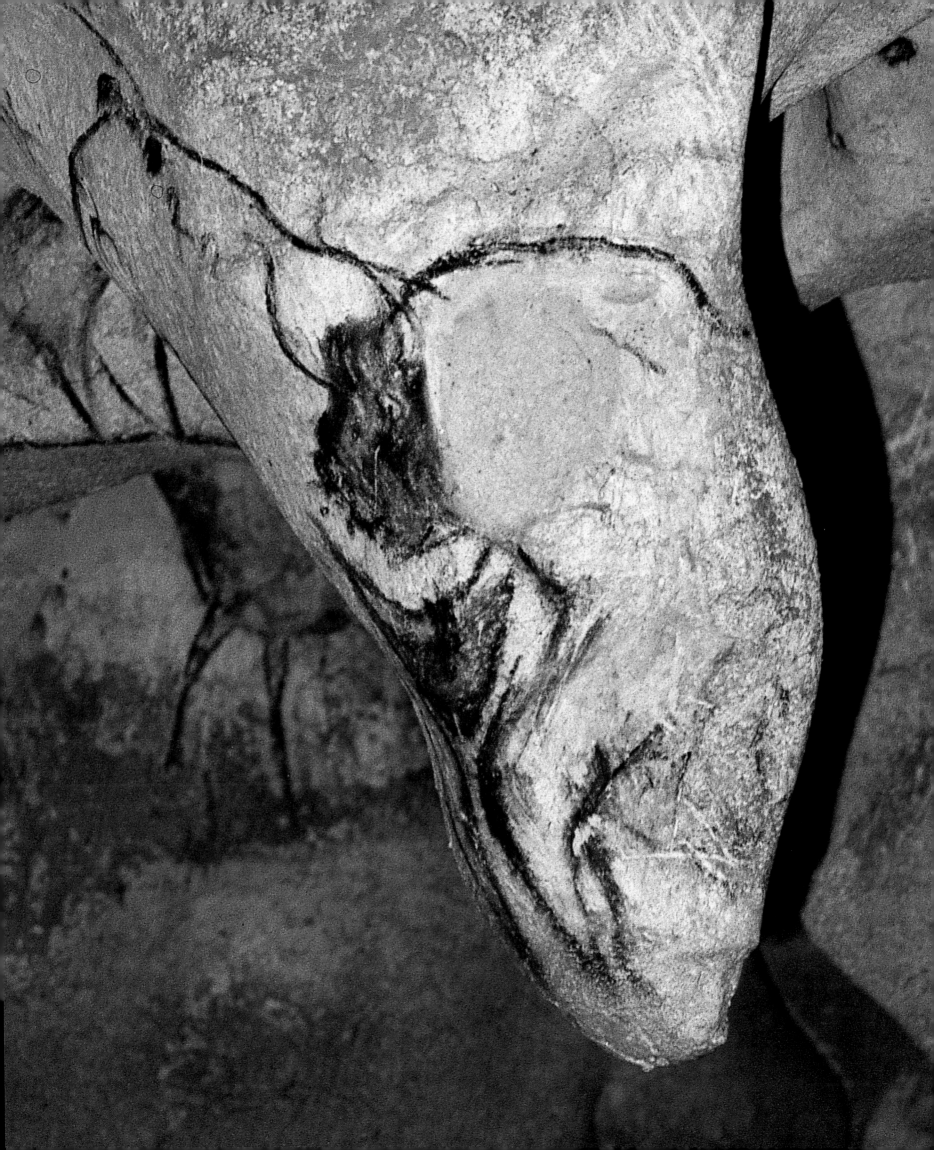

period, which must be very ancient, and are far older than had been expected.

The surprise caused by these very old dates illustrates the limits of our knowledge about Palaeolithic wall art, and underlines the danger of making chronological attributions based only on stylistic criteria, as well as the problem of the duration or recurrence of conventions. The necessity of obtaining a *series* of dates to establish a chronological evaluation, directly from the paintings or indirectly when carried out on the immediate archaeological environment, has been emphatically confirmed: a single date of around 31,000 BP would have aroused general disbelief.

These new dates overturn our conceptions not only concerning Chauvet Cave but also about the beginnings of art. Many new questions are going to arise. For example, there are some resemblances between the themes and conventions observed in Chauvet Cave and those known in various caves of the Ardèche and the Gard or elsewhere (Lascaux, Pech-Merle), as explained above. Do these resemblances mean that the artistic traditions lasted for many millennia, or that the art of these other caves is also far older than has been believed up until now? A serious revision is required.

The dominant themes in Chauvet Cave, in particular the rhinoceroses and felines, can be explained more easily now that we know that some, if not all, belong to a very remote period: over the millennia, myths and concepts must have evolved, causing changes in the choices of animals depicted. It is true that in those ancient times the ways of life remained the same and, consequently, social organization, material remains (tools, weapons, ornamentation) and *a fortiori* religious beliefs and practices changed little. However, it is natural that the Aurignacians of Chauvet viewed the world in which they lived, and that of the spirits and gods they worshipped, differently from the Magdalenians of Niaux (around 13,000 BP): after all, the latter are closer in time to ourselves than to the Chauvet artists!

The dominant presence of animals like rhinoceroses and felines in certain central panels is contrary to the long-accepted ideas set out in the 1960s by André Leroi-Gourhan (see below). The thematic structure of the sanctuary in Chauvet Cave is very different from the model he put forward. One must conclude that the artistic manifestations of the Palaeolithic religion varied through time not only in the choice of themes but also in the way they were set out. Similarly, the subdivision of Palaeolithic art proposed by Leroi-Gourhan, in successive styles, must be revised. His Style I, in which Chauvet Cave should be placed, was defined as archaic and very crude without any definite mural depictions,[12] and is obviously no longer adequate.

We now know that sophisticated techniques for wall art were invented by the Aurignacians at an early date. The rendering of perspective through various methods, the generalized use of shading, the outlining of animals, the reproduction of movement and reliefs, all date back more than 30,000 years.

This discovery has to be linked with the seventeen ivory statuettes which were discovered in Aurignacian layers, of comparable or even earlier dates, in the caves of Vogelherd, Geissenklösterle and Hohlenstein-Stadel in Baden-Württemberg (Swabian Jura, in south-west Germany). The subjects are the same: mammoths, felines, bison, bears, horse, rhinoceros and even a composite being (man with feline head).[13]

These comparisons have various interesting consequences. It becomes possible to envisage a commonality of beliefs between the Aurignacians of the Ardèche and those of the Swabian Jura (and elsewhere?). In this regard, one may speculate as to whether there were direct contacts at that time between the Ardèche and south-west Germany, via the valleys of the Rhône and the Rhine which constituted ideal thoroughfares. Moreover, the existence of remarkable portable art in the Aurignacian of Central Europe is no longer a unique phenomenon. These first

94. *The concretions of Chauvet Cave take on multiple forms, with imposing masses of stalagmites, but also some long, slender, fistulous stalactites.*

European *Homo sapiens sapiens* not only knew how to work ivory and make beautiful statuettes from it, but they also had a full mastery of graphic techniques and were just as competent at producing wall art.

This means that the Aurignacians, who coexisted with the last Neanderthals before replacing them, had artistic capabilities identical to those of their successors. Art did not have a linear evolution from clumsy and crude beginnings, as has been believed since the work of the abbé Henri Breuil. In the course of the Upper Palaeolithic, there were doubtless numerous beginnings, pinnacles and declines.[14] But from the start there were very great artists and accomplished productions in certain regions, without the situation necessarily being the same everywhere at the same time. Our view of the beginnings of artistic creation and even of the psyche of these first modern humans has been changed by this.[15]

Finally, the present absence of art before the start of the Upper Palaeolithic poses a problem, because *Homo sapiens sapiens* is known in the Near East between 90,000 and 100,000 years ago.[16] Rather than invoke a late invention of art, prepared by an immense period of trial and error, it now seems more logical – since the capabilities existed – to envisage the probability of developed forms of art which have not survived[17] or which have not yet been found. If art was indeed invented, in various different forms, several tens of thousands of years ago, one must expect new discoveries, at even older dates than those known today, between western Europe and the Near East.[18]

THE ORIGINALITY OF CHAUVET CAVE

Chauvet Cave is such a major discovery that it has caused great shock waves, even among non-specialists. There are several reasons for this. The first is the range of animals depicted, especially the rhinoceroses, lions and bears. Generally, the animals drawn in the Palaeolithic caves are hunted animals, even if their ratios in no way coincide with the hunting tallies known from excavation of the living sites. Here, the dangerous animals, which did not form part of the Palaeolithic menu, constitute the great majority (60% of the identified animals, if one adds the mammoth). This is a unique situation. The species that appear for the first time, the owl, the panther and perhaps the hyena, attract attention, but they are of more anecdotal interest, since every cave of great importance contains its share of original themes (a hare in Gabillou, a weasel in the Réseau Clastres, great auks in Cosquer).

The techniques utilized, that is to say, the way in which these animals were depicted, are also astonishing, especially through the constant use of shading and the quest for perspective, whether it be animals overlapping, bison heads on both sides of a ridge (plate 83), or even a bison whose head is seen full-face on one surface of a dihedron, while its body is perpendicular to it on the other surface (plate 88). These refinements contrast sharply with the images to which we are accustomed.

The aesthetic quality in the production of the individual works, as well as in their layout in the form of compositions full of force and life, also emphasizes the feeling of originality. As we have seen, everything was not done at the same time, and several 'hands' can be detected from the outset. Nevertheless, a large number of black paintings are so alike that they are certainly the work of a single great artist, a master draughtsperson, unless this artist was accompanied by certain people – acolytes or helpers – who used the same conventions and techniques.

The location of Chauvet Cave in the Ardèche changes our perspective on decorated caves. Until now, it was thought that there were major centres for cave art – the Périgord-Quercy region, the Pyrenees, the Cantabrian coast – and that the rest comprised minor groups like the Ardèche, the Meseta and the south of Spain, the south of Italy, plus a few caves scattered here and there. The discovery in the Ardèche, following that of Cosquer Cave, illustrates the extent of our ignorance, since original caves of the highest importance can still emerge in regions outside the great centres. With Chauvet, the Ardèche takes its place among the 'classics' of Palaeolithic wall art. The new cave also contradicts certain aspects of the theories of André Leroi-Gourhan which have been in force for thirty years.[19] He had noticed that the most frequent animals in Palaeolithic wall art – bovines and horses – were grouped in the central panels, while the rare animals such as the rhinoceroses, felines and bears were only found in marginal areas, for example at the ends of galleries. However, he had been astonished by the presence of the felines in the central panels of Bayol and La Baume-Latrone, in the Gard region of the Ardèche group.[20] Chauvet Cave reveals that big cats played an unsuspected and important role in the local bestiary, which poses the problem of their interpretation.

These animals doubtless symbolized danger, strength and power. But Chauvet Cave was a bear cave, a fact which its first prehistoric explorers could not help but notice. The bear was present through its clawmarks, its hollows, its prints, its impressive skeletons, perhaps even its odour. Is it possible that they tried to capture the essence of its power and that of animals that were comparable to it through the danger they represented and the domination they exerted over their environment? All speculations about this problem can only be guesses.

CONCLUSIONS

Chauvet Cave is very clearly one of the great sanctuaries of Palaeolithic art, comparable to Lascaux, Altamira, Les Trois-Frères or Niaux, but doubtless far more ancient. It has a decisive advantage over these caves, however, in that its floors are perfectly preserved and capable of yielding tremendous information about the human and animal activities which occurred in the cave.

The priorities, as they were set out first by Jacques Toubon, Minister of Culture, during his press conference in Paris on 18 January 1995, and later by the then Prime Minister, Edouard Balladur, on 14 February 1995 at Vallon-Pont-d'Arc, are therefore clear: the cave's conservation is paramount. It is vital that this cave be studied not only in the immediate future but also in the following decades. This means that the cave will not be open to the public. It also means that the studies and more importantly the research into the evidence will not interfere with either the images or the vulnerable floors. The second priority is research. This cave is still insufficiently documented. It will take several years before we have reliable picture counts available, exhaustive tracings, detailed studies of the phases of execution or the techniques – in short, before we shall understand a little better what happened in this cave and the intentions of the people who painted it.

In third place comes the dissemination of information. A first stage has been passed, that of making documents and information available to the public 'hot off the press'. The following stage will be the production of films, books, exhibitions, even facsimiles. It goes without saying that this will only be possible once the cave and its floors have been effectively protected and research has informed us what they represent. Only then can the caves be reproduced intelligently in the form of images or replicas. Perhaps, in this day and age when everything moves so quickly and we would like to have everything and see everything instantly, some people may regret the time that all this will take. But such an exceptional and significant discovery deserves all the precautions we can take. After all, if it has waited for thirty thousand years, what are a few years more?

127

NOTES TO THE EPILOGUE

1. ALTUNA, J., APELLANIZ, J-M., BARANDIARAN, I. 1993. *Estudio de las pinturas de Zubialde (Alava). resumen de los resultados*. Vitoria-Gasteiz, Diputación foral de Alava.
2. CLOTTES, J. and COURTIN, J. 1996. *The Cave Beneath the Sea: Paleolithic Images at Cosquer*. New York, Harry N. Abrams.
3. CLOTTES, J. and SIMONNET, R. 1972. Le réseau René Clastres de la caverne de Niaux (Ariège). *Bulletin de la Société Préhistorique française* 69 (1): 293–323. CLOTTES, J. 1995. *Les Cavernes de Niaux. Art préhistorique en Ariège*. Paris, Ed. du Seuil.
4. LEROI-GOURHAN, A. and ALLAIN, J. (eds.) 1979. *Lascaux Inconnu*. Paris, Ed. du CNRS.
5. CLOTTES, J. 1992. L'archéologie des grottes ornées. *La Recherche* 239, Vol. 23: 52–61.
6. COMBIER, J. 1984. Grottes ornées de l'Ardèche. *Les Dossiers, Histoire et Archéologie* No. 87: 80–86.
7. COMBIER, J. 1984. Grotte de la Tête-du-Lion, in *L'Art des Cavernes*, p. 598. Paris, Ministry of Culture/Imprimerie Nationale.
8. COMBIER, J. 1984. Grottes ornées de l'Ardèche. *Les Dossiers, Histoire et Archéologie* No. 87: 85.
9. COMBIER, J., DROUOT, E., HUCHARD, P. 1958. Les grottes solutréennes à gravures pariétales du Canyon inférieur de l'Ardèche. *Mémoires de la Société Préhistorique française* Vol. V: 61–117.
10. COMBIER, J. 1993. Faits nouveaux sur l'art pariétal de l'Ardèche (Résumé), in *La Protección y Conservación del Arte Rupestre paleolítico*, Servicio de Publicaciones del Principio de Asturias, p. 13.
11. FORTEA PEREZ, J., personal communication.
12. LEROI-GOURHAN, A. 1967. *The Art of Prehistoric Man*, London, Thames and Hudson, p. 148.
13. HAHN, J. 1986. *Kraft und Aggression. Die Botschaft der Eiszeitkunst im Aurignacien Süddeutschlands?* Verlag Archaeologica Venatoria, Institut für Urgeschichte der Universität Tübingen. KOZLOWSKI, J-K. 1992. *L'Art de la préhistoireen Europe orientale*. Paris, CNRS.
14. UCKO, P.J. 1987. Débuts illusoires dans l'étude de la tradition artistique. *Bulletin de la Société Préhistorique Ariège Pyrénées* 42: 15–81.
15. CLOTTES, J. 1993. La naissance du sens artistique. *Revue des Sciences morales et politiques*, pp. 173–84.
16. VALLADAS, H., REYSS, J-L., VALLADAS, G., BAR YOSEF, O., VANDERMEERSCH, B. 1988. Thermoluminescence dating of Mousterian 'Proto-Cro-Magnon' remains from Israel and the origin of modern man. *Nature* 331: 614–616.
17. BEDNARIK, R.G. 1994. A taphonomy of palaeoart. *Antiquity* 68: 68–74.
18. CLOTTES, J., CHAUVET, J-M., BRUNEL-DESCHAMPS, E., HILLAIRE, C., DAUGAS, J-P., ARNOLD, M., CACHIER, H., EVIN, J., FORTIN, P., OBERLIN, C., TISNERAT, N., VALLADAS, H. 1995. Les peintures paléolithiques de la Grotte Chauvet-Pont d'Arc, à Vallon-Pont-d'Arc (Ardèche, France): datations directes et indirectes par la méthode du radiocarbone. *Comptes rendus de l'Académie des Sciences de Paris* 320, série II a: 1133–1140. CLOTTES, J. 1995. L'originalité de la Grotte Chauvet-Pont d'Arc, à Vallon-Pont-d'Arc (Ardèche). *Revue des Sciences morales et politiques* (in press).
19. LEROI-GOURHAN, A. 1967. *The Art of Prehistoric Man*, London, Thames and Hudson.
20. LEROI-GOURHAN, A. 1967. *The Art of Prehistoric Man*, London, Thames and Hudson, p. 82.

FURTHER READING

Altuna, J., Apellániz, J. M., and Barandiarán, I. 1992. *Estudio de las Pinturas de Zubialde (Alava)*. *Resumen de los resultados*. Typescript, 71 pp. Diputación foral de Alava, Vitoria-Gasteiz.

Bahn, P.G. 1993. The 'dead wood stage' of prehistoric art studies: style is not enough, in *Rock Art Studies: The Post-Stylistic Era* or *Where do we go from here?* (M. Lorblanchet and P.G. Bahn, eds.), 51–59. Oxford, Oxbow monograph 35.

Bahn, P.G. 1995. Lascaux: Composition or accumulation? *Zephyrus* 47 (in press).

Bahn, P.G. and Vertut, J. 1988. *Images of the Ice Age*. Leicester, Windward; New York, Facts on File.

Bednarik, R.G. 1994. A taphonomy of palaeoart. *Antiquity* 68: 68–74.

Bednarik, R.G. 1994a. Conceptual pitfalls in Palaeolithic rock art dating. *Préhistoire Anthropologie Méditerranéennes* 3: 95–102.

Clottes, J. 1992. L'archéologie des grottes ornées. *La Recherche* 239, Vol. 23: 52–61.

Clottes, J. 1993. La naissance du sens artistique. *Revue des Sciences morales et politiques*, pp. 173–84.

Clottes, J. 1995. *Les Cavernes de Niaux. Art préhistorique en Ariège*. Paris, Le Seuil.

Clottes, J. 1995a. Rhinos and Lions and Bears (Oh, My!). *Natural History* May, 30–35.

Clottes, J. 1995b. L'originalité de la Grotte Chauvet-Pont d'Arc, à Vallon-Pont-d'Arc (Ardèche). *Revue des Sciences morales et politiques* (in press).

Clottes, J. and Courtin, J. 1996. *The Cave Beneath the Sea: Paleolithic Images at Cosquer*. New York, Harry N. Abrams.

Clottes, J. and Simonnet, R. 1972. Le réseau René Clastres de la caverne de Niaux (Ariège). *Bulletin de la Société Préhistorique française* 69 (1): 293–323.

Clottes, J., Chauvet, J-M., Brunel Deschamps, E., Hillaire, C., Daugas, J-P., Arnold, M., Cachier, H., Evin, J., Fortin, P., Oberlin, C., Tisnerat, N. and Valladas, H. 1995. Les peintures paléolithiques de la Grotte Chauvet-Pont d'Arc, à Vallon-Pont-d'Arc (Ardèche, France): datations directes et indirectes par la méthode du radiocarbone. *Comptes rendus de l'Académie des Sciences de Paris* 320, série II a: 1133–1140.

Clottes, J., Courtin, J., Valladas, H., Cachier, H., Mercier, N. and Arnold, M. 1992. La Grotte Cosquer datée. *Bulletin de la Société Préhistorique française* 89: 230–234.

Clottes, J., Valladas, H., Cachier, H. and Arnold, M. 1992. Des dates pour Niaux et Gargas. *Bulletin de la Société Préhistorique française* 89: 270–274.

Combier, J. 1984. Grottes ornées de l'Ardèche. *Les Dossiers, Histoire et Archéologie* No. 87: 80–86.

Combier, J. 1984a. Grotte de la Tête-du-Lion, in *L'Art des Cavernes*, p. 598. Paris, Ministry of Culture/Imprimerie Nationale.

Combier, J. 1993. Faits nouveaux sur l'art pariétal de l'Ardèche (Résumé), in *La Protección y Conservación del Arte Rupestre paleolítico*, Servicio de Publicaciones del Principio de Asturias, p. 13.

Combier, J., Drouot, E. and Huchard, P. 1958. Les grottes solutréennes à gravures pariétales du Canyon inférieur de l'Ardèche. *Mémoires de la Société Préhistorique française* Vol. V: 61–117.

Groupe de Réflexion sur l'Art Pariétal Paléolithique 1993. *L'Art Pariétal Paléolithique. Techniques et Méthodes d'Etudes*. Paris, Edition du Comité des Travaux Historiques et Scientifiques.

Hahn, J. 1986. *Kraft und Aggression. Die Botschaft der Eiszeitkunst im Aurignacien Süddeutschlands?* Verlag Archaeologica Venatoria, Institut für Urgeschichte der Universität Tübingen.

Igler, W., Dauvois, M., Hyman, M., Menu, M., Rowe, M., Vézian, J. and Walter, P. 1994. Datation radiocarbone de deux figures pariétales de la grotte du Portel (Commune de Loubens, Ariège). *Bulletin de la Société Préhistorique Ariège-Pyrénées* 49: 231–236.

Kozlowski, J-K. 1992. *L'Art de la préhistoire en Europe orientale*. Paris, CNRS.

Landon, V. 1995 Qui a peint la Grotte de Zubialde? *Science et Vie Junior*, Dossier Hers Série, Les Hommes Préhistoriques, No. 22, October, 84–89.

Leroi-Gourhan, A. 1967. The Art of Prehistoric Man. London, Thames and Hudson.

Leroi-Gourhan, A. and Allain, J. (eds.) 1979. *Lascaux Inconnu*. Paris, CNRS.

Lorblanchet, M. 1993. From styles to dates, in *Rock Art Studies: The Post-Stylistic Era* or *Where do we go from here?* (M. Lorblanchet and P.G. Bahn, eds.), 61–72. Oxford, Oxbow monograph 35.

Marshack, A. 1995. Images of the Ice Age. *Archaeology* 48 (4) (July/August): 28–39.

Puech, P-F. and Albertini, H. 1995. L'ours, la lionne qui n'en était pas une, et le préhistorien. *La Recherche* 26, No. 279: 872–873.

Ucko, P.J. 1987. Débuts illusoires dans l'étude de la tradition artistique. *Bulletin de la Société Préhistorique Ariège-Pyrénées* 42: 15–81.

Valladas, H., Cachier, H., Maurice, P., Bernaldo de Quiros, F., Clottes, J., Cabrera Valdés, V., Uzquiano, P. and Arnold, M. 1992. Direct radiocarbon dates for prehistoric paintings at the Altamira, El Castillo and Niaux caves. *Nature* 357: 68–70.

CHRONOLOGY

Chronological chart of cave drawings directly dated by radiocarbon, in years before the present (BP):

Chauvet (Ardèche): right-hand facing rhino: 32,410 + 720 (Gif A 95132)
                                                 30,790 + 600 (Gif A 95133)
Chauvet (Ardèche): left-hand facing rhino: 30,940 + 610 (Gif A 95126)
Chauvet (Ardèche): bison: 30,340 + 570 (Gif A 95128)
Cosquer (Bouches-du Rhône): hand stencil: 27,110 + 390 (Gif A 92409)
                                                 27,110 + 350 (Gif A 92491)
Cougnac (Lot): female megaceros: 25,120 + 390 (Gif A 92425)
Pech-Merle (Lot): right-hand spotted horse: 24,640 + 390 (Gif A 95357)
Cougnac (Lot): male megaceros: 23,610 + 350 (Gif A 91183)
                                                 22,750 + 390 (Gif A 92426)
Cougnac (Lot): female megaceros: 19,500 + 270 (Gif A 91324)
Cosquer (Bouches-du Rhône): feline: 19,200 + 220 (Gif A 92418)
Cosquer (Bouches-du Rhône): horse: 18,840 + 240 (Gif A 92416)
                                                 18,820 + 310 (Gif A 92417
Cosquer (Bouches-du Rhône): bison   18,530 + 180 (Gif A 92492)
                                                 18,010 + 190 (Gif A 92419)
Altamira (Santander): large bison facing right: 14,330 + 190 (Gif A 91181)
Cougnac (Lot): black dot: 14,290 + 180 (Gif A 89250
La Covaciella (Asturias): bison: 14,260 + 130 (Gif A 95364)
La Covaciella (Asturias): bison: 14,060 + 140 (Gif A 95281)
Altamira (Santander): large bison facing left: 13,940 + 170 (Gif A 91179)
Niaux (Ariège): bison, panel 5:   13,850 + 150 (Gif A 92501)
Cougnac (Lot): black fingermark: 13,810 + 210 (Gif A 92500)
Altamira (Santander): small bison facing left: 13,570 + 190 (Gif A 91178)
El Castillo (Santander): large bison facing right: 13,060 + 200 (Gif A 91004)
Niaux (Ariège): black line, panel 1:   13,060 + 200 (Gif A 92499)
El Castillo (Santander): large bison facing right: 12,910 + 180 (Gif A 91172)
Niaux (Ariège): bison, panel 1:   12,890 + 160 (Gif A 91319)
Le Portel (Ariège): Niaux-type horse: 12,180 + 125 (AA 9465)
Le Portel (Ariège): big horse: 11,600 + 150 (AA 9766)

INDEX

134